D1516258

THE HARDEST JOURNEY HOME

DONLEIGH O. GAUNKY

THE HARDEST JOURNEY HOME

A True Story of Loss and Duty
During the Iraq War

WESTHOLME
Yardley

©2017 Donleigh O. Gaunky

All rights reserved under International and Pan-American Copyright Conventions. No part of this book may be reproduced in any form or by any electronic or mechanical means, including information storage and retrieval systems, without permission in writing from the publisher, except by a reviewer who may quote brief passages in a review.

Westholme Publishing, LLC
904 Edgewood Road
Yardley, Pennsylvania 19067
Visit our Web site at www.westholmepublishing.com

ISBN: 978-1-59416-291-6
Also available as an eBook.

Printed in the United States of America.

"It is also true, however, that whatever their fond sentiments for men and women in uniform, for most Americans the wars remain an abstraction. A distant and unpleasant series of news items that does not affect them personally."

—Secretary of Defense Robert Gates,
Duke University, September 29, 2010

Contents

Introduction

This book has taken a long time to get to this point. Its inception began not long after the events described in it. Over time, the idea of merely writing this story became something that I rebelled against. Not because I didn't want the story told, or that it was an unimportant story. No, it was because of my own views of it. The events in this book are a snapshot. They don't represent the totality of what happened during my time in military service, and I saw a need to write a more complete story of that era in my life. This, despite many people telling me that this particular story was more than enough not only to hold people's attention, but to captivate, to introduce them to something they had never even considered before—at least not during this generation's tenure into military conflict and war. One of the more impressionable attempts to get me to write this book was from my father, who had to deal with these events himself from a different perspective. He encouraged me to put this set of days and the events onto paper. For a long time, having made up my mind to not just describe one incident, I resisted his and other's encouragement. Only after long consideration, I came to understand that this particular story not only met my initial want to write about my military service, but I was now at a place in my life when I could do so, with as much detail—certainly more than had been expressed before—as I could bring to bear.

More importantly, I came to realize a need in the books of today's wars to put forth something that should have been an unlikely, some might say impossible, scenario. It should have been so due to policies and procedures put into place after significant family losses, such as the Sullivan brothers and the Niland brothers of the World War II era, became much more public through mass media. The possibility that in today's military an entire generation of a family could enlist, or be commissioned, into service and potentially be killed off wholesale, seems improbable to most. It would seem even more unlikely that even a part of a single generation of one family could be at war at the same time, where the risk of death to one of them would be in itself a tragedy. The possibility that a sibling, engaged in the same conflict with other siblings, could be called upon to bring one of their siblings home from the battlefield in a flag-encased box is something one could only think possible in a Hollywood movie. In the HBO film "Taking Chance," actor Kevin Bacon's character comes into contact with another "remains escort" who, as he would find out, is the brother of the soldier he is accompanying home. The film is based on a true story, but that particular scene is, regrettably, a work of Hollywood in order to bring a greater sense of impact and loss to the overall story. And it frustrated me when I finally learned that particular fact, for after seeing that film, and given the events of the story you are shortly to read, I tried for more than a few years to find that individual, as I felt that they were the only other person who would know the same kind of challenge, heartbreak, and reality that I had come to know. Finding myself to be largely alone in the aftermath of learning the truth of that particular story, I resolved to come back and do this story as I had originally intended to mere months after I had lived these events more than a decade ago. So, unlike that scene in a movie that is hard to watch more than once for even the strongest willed of individuals, the story that follows is no work of fiction. It is real. It is one that I find, now more than ever with the events going on in the world, needs to be told, for I fear what I have had to endure, both in the events below and in putting this story to paper, is merely just the beginning of more sorrows to come.

Author's Note: I have attempted to put conversations into the book to the best of my ability, or to at least present the tone of such discussions. Any errors that have occurred regarding conversations or the exact timeline of events are mine, and mine alone.

Prologue

It was a fairly brisk morning in which Dad, Alex, and I had a quick breakfast before heading over to the nearby town of Tomah, Wisconsin, and the AMTRAK station. For Alex this trip marked the end of a needed leave before he began his first deployment to the Middle East. For me, it was my second full day on leave before I made my own return to the same region. For the moment, though, it was just the three of us waiting for the train that would bring Alex down to relatives near the northern Chicago suburbs for a day or so before he returned to Fort Campbell, Kentucky. Within minutes of our arrival, Alex's fiancée and her parents pulled into the little parking lot of the small station. Alex went over to her, and they spent the next hour or so being as close to one another as they could. Dad and I met and shook hands with what we presumed would be our in-laws after Alex came back from this deployment. The conversations between us were small, talking about such things as the weather, gas prices, and whatever else struck us as something of interest while we waited for the train. An hour and a half after we arrived, the loud, unmistakable sound of a passenger train could be heard. We watched as the AMTRAK train started to slow to a stop, its wheels screeching along the tracks. I approached Alex for some last minute encouragement.

"Hey man, keep your head down okay, and listen to your NCOs (Non-commissioned officers)."

"Yeah, yeah, I know. I know," he replied. We hugged, and I left him with the others to say their goodbyes. Within five minutes, Alex was on the train and out of view.

It was the end of a couple of days at the beginning of my pre-deployment leave, and the last of Alex's. Despite this brief overlap, we managed to have some good times. Alex and I took several pictures with family, a few of which included both of us in uniform. At Mom's house a little over a day and a half before, it had been photos in our military dress uniforms, our "Class A's" as the army calls them. I even managed to convince Alex to turn so that we had our shoulders to each other. He had his left shoulder to the camera, I had my right. On both was the renowned unit patch of the historic 101st "Screaming Eagles" Airborne Division (Air Assault). Alex's patch on the left shoulder meant that he was part of the 101st now, while they were preparing for their latest deployment. My patch, on my right shoulder, meant that I'd been with them previously, during a period of conflict. In fact, it had been only a little over six months before when I'd worn that famous patch on both shoulders, signifying my being in the unit, and having gone to war with it. I knew that in the not too distant future, Alex would have that same reality, that same pride and honor, that same legacy.

Alex Gaunky, left, and the author during their leave in 2005. (*Author*)

The night before Alex left, we had our duty/combat uniforms on. Alex had on the newly issued Army Combat Uniform (ACU), the digital camouflage uniforms most associated with the wars in Iraq and Afghanistan. I was in my Desert Camouflage Uniform (DCU), the multi-tan-colored uniform that was the step up from those worn by soldiers in Desert Storm. It was weird to have two different uniforms that were going to be intertwined by units going into Iraq and Afghanistan in that fall of 2005. Earlier that same day, Alex and I went with our Dad to visit our relative everyone called either Harry or "Cousin" Harry, who was our grandfather's first cousin. He too was a member of the 101st Airborne, but from a time long since past; he was part of the 506th Parachute Infantry Regiment made so famous by Stephen Ambrose's book *Band of*

Two generations of 101st Airborne, from left to right, Cousin Harry, World War II veteran, Alex, and the author.

Brothers and the miniseries that came out of it. We even got a picture of the three of us together, three 101st soldiers, of different eras, different campaigns, and different wars. It was a day I won't soon forget.

But these were memories of the previous two days, when Alex and I had time to talk. Now he was on a train, heading to spend no more than a day or two with other relatives down near Chicago, before going back to Fort Campbell, and then on to his combat tour in Iraq.

I would have one more conversation with Alex via phone after this, but this was the last time I would ever see him alive. I didn't know it at the time. If I had, I would have said a lot more than the stereotypical big brother or fellow soldier sentiments, but that was not to be.

ONE

WARNO

17 November 2005
Corps Analysis and Control Element,
Camp Victory, Baghdad, Iraq

"You're in early," Sergeant Robinson, my daytime counterpart, said as I walked into the office from the dining facility about an hour before my twelve-hour overnight shift.

"Yeah, wanted to get a head start, as well as check on any emails I may have gotten over the shift," I replied.

"Ah," Sergeant Robinson returned. "I'm guessing that means you'll want access to the NIPRNet computer then." (NIPRNet is the Non-Secure, Internet Protocol Router Network, where unclassified information, such as emails between soldiers, can be sent and read.)

"If it's available, yeah, otherwise, I'll just start looking at the SIGACTs (Significant Activities)."

"Why the SIGACTs?" Robinson asked, somewhat curious as to why I would even need to look at those.

"Just something Captain Bryant asked us to start looking at daily. I've already been reading them every shift anyway, so it's not a big deal."

"OK," Sergeant Robinson said, and then went back to what she was working on while I went over to the classified computer and started reading the SIGACT database reports.

For a while, all that could be heard was the idle chit-chat of the day shift crew as they got ready to finish their tasks for the day and give those of us on night duty a shift change brief before turning operations over to us. The SIGACTs were what I expected them to be, a listing of different bombings and small engagements around the country, including those just to the east of us in the capital city of Baghdad. As I started to get to the acts that had happened as I had come off shift almost twelve hours earlier, I saw one with the following description:

SVBIED (Suicide Vehicle-Borne Improvised Explosive Device, aka Car Bomb)/Hostile Vehicle Accident?

Yes, there was a question mark included in the event title, as though those who had submitted the event weren't sure what it really was, and as such, to cover all possible bases, they put all reported possibilities. I clicked on the event, which occurred at a little after 7 a.m. local that morning, and saw designations for one of the units in the 101st. Noted in the act was the designator for Alex's unit. It was the first time I'd seen his unit come up in a SIGACT, and I immediately took stock of the situation by reading it a couple of times. My biggest concern on reading it was that it had the following battle damage assessment, or put simply, the casualties and equipment losses: One soldier had been killed in the event, two others had been severely injured. At this point, the pit of my stomach began to feel heavy. Worry began to grow in my mind, even though there was no way for sure I could know that Alex had even been part of this event. Somehow, that didn't matter, my mind was telling me something was wrong, and that something had happened to Alex.

I was about ready to go to the unclassified system when one of my fellow night shift personnel, Specialist Rodgers, came by and said, "Hey, they're about to start the shift change brief."

I nodded and turned my chair around to listen to what those on day shift had for us, and left the computer on the SIGACT screen, ready to go back to it when the handover was done. The handover briefing took about fifteen minutes. Nothing out of the ordinary, no flare-ups in activity, at least so far, nothing but the usual missions and requirements. As soon as the briefing ended, I turned my chair around and reviewed the SIGACT twice more before I went over to the unclassified system. After logging on with the proper credentials, I pulled up a web browser and went straight to the internal army email site of the time, called Army Knowledge Online, or AKO. Think of it like a supercharged version of Microsoft Outlook. I put in Alex's army email address and sent him a message. The basics of that message were these: "Let me know you're okay. I don't need to know any details, I know you can't give them to me anyway. Just let me know that you're okay."

After ensuring that the message transmission was successful, I logged off the site, and went straight into work, creating the day's news list and working on a powerpoint slide to go into the following morning's briefing to the commanding general of Multinational Corp-Iraq, which at the time was Lieutenant General Vines, the commander of XVIII Airborne Corps, the military unit with overall day-to-day operations in Iraq.

I'd sent Alex the message around 7:30 p.m. Every half hour or so, I would take a quick break away from work, go back to the unclassified computer, log into AKO, and see if Alex had replied. And every time that I didn't see a message, I would try to rationalize why it wasn't there. Alex was off shift. Or perhaps he didn't have immediate access to the internet. These were the thoughts going through my head while I waited and worked. The one that didn't enter my head, the one that should have, the one that, having dealt with a similar situation before at a lower level of organization, was that the unit had cut off communication to the outside world so that any family impacted by the actions could be notified through proper military channels. That thought never even crossed my mind. It never even made a hint of an appearance.

After an hour and a half at work, periodically checking my emails, I decided again to see if Alex had responded. Once again, I logged onto my AKO account. Once again, there was no response back from Alex. There was, however, an email from my father. I clicked on it to open it up. It's salutations and first line will forever be burned into my memory.

"Hi Don,
This is a letter I hoped I'd never have to write . . . ."

It didn't take long for me to read through the rest of it, very aware of what I was about to read from that first line. The letter described that Alex had been in an incident, and I knew almost immediately what it was. Dad further went on to say that Alex had a severe head wound, and that they were moving him to Landstuhl Regional Medical Center (LRMC) in Germany for further treatment. After I finished reading the email, I forwarded it to my local unclassified account, forwarded it again to my older brother Dave, or at least the last email I had of his on file as he was out on a navy vessel in the midst of his own second tour in the Persian Gulf, and then logged off. I pulled up my local Outlook account, and looked for Staff Sergeant Thai, my immediate supervisor, as well as Captain Bryant, my officer-in-charge (OIC), and forwarded the email I had just forwarded to myself from Dad. I then went over to the classified system, found the SIGACT, and sent a link to it to that same pair, so that they would know as much as I did about what was going on. I then closed out the browser, and turned to Rodgers.

"I'm gonna go outside for a few minutes for some air." I'm not sure if I looked pale or gave off an air of concern. I also didn't look back to get a response after I told him I was going outside. I just moved through the cavernous path in the building to an entrance in the back, not far from our office, where I finally caught my breath, and the reality of what I was going to have to deal with in terms of my little brother being, at that point, severely injured. My arms shook violently. It wasn't a cold night either, so I knew enough that this was a sign of my body going into, most likely, a state of shock. I stayed outside for about five minutes or so, numb, my thoughts blank. When I was sure the shaking had subsided enough for me to get back inside and go back to work to help distract my mind, I did so. I went back to my desk and just continued working on finding an article for the PowerPoint slide I needed to get done, and worked on the MS Word document so that it could be disbursed before the morning update. Little did I know that I wouldn't be at work for much longer that evening.

I had been back at my desk for maybe a half hour when my boss's superior, Major Baude, a man for whom I have immense respect, stopped on the other side of the cubical-like wall that bordered the back side of my desk.

"Sergeant Gaunky, are you okay?" He'd been told by Captain Bryant about the two emails I'd sent her, and felt the need to come see how I was doing. I don't recall responding in any particular way, as I was still in somewhat of a state of shock. Following my nonspecific response, he set down his satellite phone on my desk.

"Here," he said, followed by—presumably seeing a somewhat confused look on my face—"Make sure that you take some time to call your folks. They'll probably want to hear from you. You can bring the phone back to Captain Bryant when you're done, and she'll get it back to me."

"Thank you sir," was all I responded, and as he walked away, I went back to work. After twenty minutes, I came to the realization that the major was correct, and I let Specialist Rodgers and my immediate boss, Staff Sergeant Thai, know that I was going outside to call my folks. Both acknowledged my sentiment, and let me take my leave. I stepped back outside, made sure I was by myself and away from prying ears, and started my first of two phone calls.

"Hey Dad, it's me, Don. I got your message," were the first words out of my mouth after I finished hearing my Dad's answering machine message. My Dad is one who normally screens his calls, so there is no way to know for sure if he will pick up or not.

"Don, good to hear you got it," he replied after he knew it was me and picked up the phone.

"Yeah. Any idea how bad Alex is?" No point in beating around the bush, straight and to the point.

"Not good, from what I can tell. I was contacted by the Doc who was working on him over there, and we talked about what he knew. I asked him for his honest assessment about Alex. From the sounds of it, it's pretty bad."

"So, do you know if they're moving him out of theater, or what you guys are going to be doing when you find out what is going to happen?"

"They're moving him out sometime soon to the military hospital in Germany. The government officials who contacted us sound like they are going to expedite the process to get us passports to get there to see him."

I followed shortly with, "Well, I would imagine that something might happen on my end as well that gets me over there. I'll try to keep you and Mom in the loop from my end on anything in that regard."

"Sounds good," he replied. A few more things were spoken between us before I hung up and made my second call, this time to Mom. My parents had been divorced for several years at that point.

"Hey Mom, it's me, Don."

"Hi Don," my Mom said with melancholy and sadness in her voice. "I'm guessing you heard about Alex then." Small sniffs could be heard coming from her side of the phone.

"Yeah, Dad sent me an email about it."

"That's good," she replied.

"I hear the government is trying to get you guys expedited passports," I state, trying to get whatever information I could from my Mom, as well as to be able to gauge where she was emotionally, as I knew that for myself, at this point, even while talking with family, I was numb and on autopilot.

"Yes, we're working on getting copies of Bob's and my birth certificates from Illinois so that we can get them done as soon as possible."

"How is Bob holding up?" Bob is my twin brother, who was living in the same city as my Mom at that time. He'd been out of the navy for a little over a year, was working at Applebee's, and finalizing his requirements to start college the following year. While in the navy, he'd done a deployment to the Middle East.

"He's shaken up. But then again, we all kind of are at this point."

"Yeah, I know the feeling."

After a few more minutes of discussion, including a recommendation on my part that Mom put in requests to the Red Cross to get a hold of both Dave and myself (as the military is a bit of a stickler on protocol when it comes to these kinds of things), to which she agreed, I ended the call and went back inside. After giving the satellite phone over to Captain Bryant, I went back to my desk and returned to work while I awaited whatever was going to happen next.

The four Gaunky brothers. Left to right: Dave, Alex, Donleigh, and Bob. (*Author*)

At some point over the next hour, I had two visitations. One by a senior noncommissioned officer attached to our unit to see how I was, as he had apparently been told of what was going on. I told him I was fine, or at least as fine as I could be given the circumstances. After our brief conversation, he left. The other visit was from my company commander, Captain Hoecherl. He came into our office in his PT uniform, minus his reflective belt. He came over to my desk.

"Sergeant Gaunky, how are you doing?"

"I'm doing okay, sir."

"Do you want to talk to a chaplain about what's going on?" I should note that my commander was considerably more religious than I was at that time, or remain today.

"No, sir, I'll be fine without."

"You sure?"

"Yes sir, I'm sure."

"Okay. Well, if you change your mind, just find me and let me know."

"If I do, sir, I will."

"Okay." With that, he left. The one thing I knew for certain at that point in time was that I didn't want to talk to a chaplain. Given that there was no indication that Alex was going to or had died at that point, I didn't see any need. Even if there had been such indications, I know I wouldn't have wanted to talk to a chaplain. I returned to work.

Some time before midnight, I was approached by my company's first sergeant, Sergeant First Class Collier, as well as the sergeant major for the department, Sergeant Major Allen, with news of what was going to happen to me.

"Sergeant Gaunky, we're going to need you to step away from work. We're working on getting you out of country to be with your brother," Sergeant Major Allen said. Sergeant Collier concurred. I got up from my chair, and turned to Specialist Rodgers.

"Hey Rodgers, I've got a good start on tonight's work. Here," I said as I pointed to the monitor, showing the slide I was working on and analyzing, "is the article for tomorrow. Pretty sure you can see where I was going on this. I'll leave it to you on how to finish it." Rodgers had been tapped to be my alternate for those nights I was either on another task or for those rare occasions I had the night off of work. More than competent in his job, I was glad command picked him to be the other guy to work on these tasks.

"Got it," was his reply, and I thanked him. I would later find out that it was Staff Sergeant Thai and Captain Bryant who had gotten the ball rolling on getting me to be with Alex. For that, I was and continue to be forever thankful to them. I then retrieved my weapon, and walked towards the back of the office to find out what the next moves would be.

The first move would be for me to go back to the "barrack" at building 51F, a warehouse that had been turned into a berthing unit for soldiers from several different units. Rather than having to walk the mile or so walk from the palace to the barracks, first sergeant, sergeant major, and I instead got into one of the vehicles under the unit's charge and drove a couple minutes to the building.

"Get what you need for your trip, and lock the rest of your equipment up in your wall locker. Also, get your basic load out so we can put that into proper storage." These were my instructions as we pulled up to the building.

I stepped out of the vehicle, and walked into the building, past the two soldiers on duty as fire guards, basically those meant to ensure proper security and safety of the building during their shift. I pulled out my flashlight, and continued on into the large bay room in which our sleeping quarters, in all their myriad configurations, were housed. It took me a couple minutes to find my particular sleeping area. It also took me a minute or two to unlock and open my wall locker, as I was trying to not wake up those sleeping in the vicinity as I fumbled with the lock.

From my wall locker I pulled out a duffel bag and stuffed it with a couple of uniforms, a set of boots, part of my multi-part sleeping bag system, a fleece jacket top, and my personal hygiene bag. I then removed the magazines of ammo that made up my basic load and pulled out my kevlar helmet and flak vest. After

I closed and locked my locker, I grabbed my duffel bag, the helmet, flak vest, basic load, and my weapon that I had taken with me from the office and went outside to the waiting vehicle. We drove back to the office, at which point I placed my weapon into the office's weapons rack, turned over my magazines of ammo to my officer in charge, and said a few goodbyes prior to taking my leave. Sometime during this period, Sergeant Major Allen had made a statement to me regarding the capabilities of the Landstuhl medical staff, likely in response to the appearance on my face, knowing what I did about the seriousness of Alex's condition.

"The people at Landstuhl are good at what they do; they've been known to perform miracles." That may have been true, but I had my doubts.

I didn't give any response to her comments, at least not verbally. After saying my last goodbyes, we went back to the vehicle. After another few minutes of driving we ended up at my unit's battalion headquarters. There was a flurry of movement in the building, with most people in their physical training uniforms, likely woken up after having been informed of my situation and working to help. I was given a place to sit and wait.

Sometime in the first hour after our arrival at the battalion headquarters, as I sat there waiting to be told what to do next, the battalion's senior enlisted soldier, the command sergeant major, came into the office in his PT uniform.

"Sergeant Gaunky," he stated, once he was sure who I was.

"Sergeant major," I replied, standing as I settled into parade rest just as all enlisted soldiers are taught to do when encountering a senior enlisted non-commissioned officer.

"At ease, Gaunky," he replied and I relaxed a little. He then proceeded with the information that I had not yet heard about what was going on with Alex. "We were going to try to get you on the same bird [plane] as your brother, but they're already preparing to move, and we're going to miss that window. So, at this point, we're working on getting you a release document and orders to fly to Kuwait with follow on orders to Landstuhl so you can meet him there."

I nodded in reply, keeping quiet as I again waited for whatever the next move would be. Sometime in the next hour, the adjutant, or senior personnel officer for the brigade, the battalion's higher headquarters, came into the office. She also apparently had been woken up upon the news of what one of the brigade's soldiers, that is, me, was going through, and got to work in expediting the paper process as quickly as she could. When she arrived, she had most of the paperwork in her hand, explaining to those of us present, including my first sergeant, that they needed to get the brigade commander's signature to officially sign off on my release. At that point, we all hopped into the same vehicle I'd been in multiple times that evening. It was still very early in the morning, and we drove for several minutes until we pulled up to a group of sleeping trailers assigned to senior personnel and married individuals during deployments. The adjutant departed from the vehicle, and went to the trailer of her superior. After a few minutes, she returned, paperwork signed, officially clearing me to be able to leave the combat theater to be with my brother. All that was left was for me to go to the departure point on the military-controlled side of Baghdad International Airport, colloquially called BIAP (by-op), and await the flight to Kuwait. Before doing so, our department sergeant major, the one who had told me about the miracles performed at Landstuhl, bid me goodbye and returned to the palace office so that she could complete her shift. After that, Sergeant Collier and I made the trek to BIAP in order for me to finish my preparation to fly out.

We arrived early enough to make a stop just outside the check-in/holding area to grab a cup of coffee from the nearby coffee shop that had been set up at the post. It was needed, as the whole night had been energy draining for a multitude of reasons for everyone. Mine had just been the waiting, which is often the hardest thing to do. Collier and I simply drank our respective caffeinated beverages, and talked about various things that, given the situation, were largely of little consequence but served enough purpose in keeping me distracted while I waited for the next move.

As per regulatory requirements, we made it to the check-in "tent" where I was supposed to ensure proper inclusion on the flight's manifest. The flight that I'd been told I was going to be on was the first one set to leave that day at approximately 8 a.m. The reality though was inherently different, as there was no 8 a.m. flight. As such, the first sergeant and I talked to the servicemembers who operate and run flight operations to get me on the actual first flight down to Kuwait that day, which turned out would not be until somewhere between 11 a.m. and 12 p.m. For the next three or four hours, I sat underneath a pavilion not far from the tent in the midst of the holding area for those traveling. My duffel bag was checked in to be placed into holding until the aircraft was ready to receive it, while I held on to my helmet and flak vest. During that time, my first sergeant kept in contact with my immediate supervisors, who

The author on the flight up to Iraq from Kuwait to begin his second deployment. (*Courtesy Brett Rodgers*)

were in touch with the people who were flying Alex up to Landstuhl. There was no change in status of whether or not he had arrived at the hospital. Right before I and a decent sized group of people were called to get into line to begin boarding the aircraft, one more call was made. After my first sergeant finished the call, she came to me and told me the results of the conversation.

"The person in charge says that your little brother has arrived at the hospital. When we asked what his status was, on your behalf, they said that you needed to contact your family."

"Well, given that we're about ready to leave, I'll have to wait to do that when I get there."

After a quick good luck sentiment shared between us, I got in line, and boarded the aircraft that was to bring us down to

Kuwait, and from there to our own destinations beyond. The aircraft I boarded was either a C-5 or C-17 aircraft, a plane considerably larger than the C-130 transport aircraft that most soldiers are used to flying in. Compared to a flight on C-130, which has cramped seating and support for soldiers, this plane had relatively comfortable seats, room for us to stretch our legs, and—given the relatively small size of our manifest—room to not have to sit next to another person if one desired. It was, given the situation, a quite comfortable way to travel in the military transport system.

I walked down the left side of the aircraft, somewhere in the middle of the "passenger" section of the plane to find a seat that was comfortable enough to keep myself occupied during the flight back down to the southern desert. A few minutes after I sat down, another soldier sat down in the seat next to me. After he settled into his seat, we got into a bit of discussion. After talking about where we were stationed in the region, within the limits of our ability to speak about our jobs, we moved on to the reasons for why we were both on this particular flight away from the war zone.

"So, I'm on my way home. You?"

"Landstuhl."

"Are you injured?"

"No, my brother was injured up north."

"Oh, sorry to hear that."

"It is what it is," I would reply, and continue to reply to such sentiments to this day.

"Still. Hope he pulls through."

"Thanks. So, what's got you going home?"

"My Mom just passed. Cancer."

"Oh man, I'm sorry to hear that," I replied. Both of us were going on what was referred to as emergency leave, which is essentially what it sounds like. When something happens where you need to go home, or in my case to Landstuhl, you are put on emergency leave orders. After this little bit of conversation, we both went on to find ways to relax. I took a bit of a nap, or at least as much of one as I could.

Around mid-afternoon, we arrived at the all-too-familiar gateway into the war zone in Kuwait. We all stepped off the aircraft and were bused to the tent terminal, followed by another bus that took us to Camp Doha, one of the major camps at that time in Kuwait for staging personnel for either going into Iraq or going home. We were taken to another tent and given a presentation on what we had to do before we were to fly out later that evening. We were also directed to the tents that would be our housing for the hours we were going to be there while we waited for our flight to depart. After this, we went to a large trailer to process our orders, and to sign out on our respective leaves. On completing this, we moved to the trailer next door to get our flight tickets. Following this, the soldier I'd met on the plane and I went to the on site storage facility to store our body armor. After getting our receipt to get our armor back, we went back to the first trailer to await our next set of directions.

After a few more minutes of waiting, we were instructed that we needed to wear civilian attire on our flights out; we were not allowed to wear our uniforms like those leaving on R&R flights. Lacking civilian attire, as our command at the time did not see a need for us to bring any (unlike my first deployment where the command made it a requirement), I had to go get some before we departed. I went with the same soldier from the plane to the local PX to get something to wear. The result was a set of khaki pants that were a couple sizes too large, but thankfully with a belt to keep them up, and a green T-shirt with a stereotypical patriotic type design. After that, with nothing else to do, we went to our designated tent to wait once again. There, just as on the plane, I took a nap, not knowing when I'd have time to get any good sleep in the days to come.

It was after dusk when a soldier came into the tent and woke everyone up to get ready to move. After dry shaving and a quick baby wipe bath, I rolled up my sleeping bag and made sure to put everything back into my duffel, except my paperwork in a folder, and moved outside to head back to the trailer office I'd been to several times that day. After a few minutes, a couple of buses came into view. We stacked up our duffels and other types of bug-out bags, placed them in the storage underneath the carriage, and climbed into the bus. After a headcount was done, the buses took off, but not toward a military aircraft. Instead, they progressed toward the Kuwait International Airport. We were walked through security before being put into a holding area to await our flight. In the remaining time, many of us grabbed something to eat or a coffee to drink within the confines of our holding area. After a while, we were moved to our respective gates, checked by security one last time, and then walked to our planes. After boarding my plane, I sat back, and tried to think of nothing else but what I would do when I got to Germany, such as seeing my parents and Alex again. Just after the flight took off, I took one more nap to pass the time as productively as I could manage.

TWO

Landstuhl

Germany and Fisher House
19 November 2005

We arrived at the airport in Frankfurt, Germany, sometime between 6 a.m. and 7 a.m. on Saturday, November 19. It was now over forty-eight hours since Alex's incident, and because I had been out of contact with anyone who could give me answers about his condition for about eighteen hours or so, I had no idea what I would be encountering when I got to the hospital. Would he be better? Would he be worse? Would he be dead? If my mind hadn't been on autopilot to get to the next point of movement, these would probably be the questions meandering through my head. As it was, I was just focused on making contact with the detachment that would get me down to Landstuhl. I walked out of the plane into the main terminal. After passing through the local customs office, in which I showed them my orders and military ID, which at that time acted as the equivalent to a passport, I moved down to baggage claim to get my bag. As I passed a security door into the baggage claim area, I could see someone with a military style haircut come towards me. This was going to be my contact in Germany.

"Sergeant Gaunky?" he asked, trying to confirm he had the right person. I nodded in reply.

"I'm the rear detachment commander. I'm here to help facilitate movement and get you to where you need to go. This . . . ," he said as he pointed to another soldier near him, both of whom, now that I got a better look, were in civilian attire, "is my driver. He'll be helping out as well."

"Nice to meet you both," I replied as I shook hands with them. We went over to the baggage carousel, picked up my duffel bag, and then walked outside. We talked for several minutes while walking to the duty vehicle. When we got there, I placed my bag into a back seat and sat down next to it, the other soldier and the rear detachment commander taking seats up front.

"How long is the trip down to Landstuhl from here?" I asked, trying to figure out a few different things in my head.

"About an hour or so," the rear detachment commander, a captain as it turned out, replied.

I merely nodded, and looked out the window as we drove from Frankfurt to Landstuhl. Beyond a few bits of conversation here and there, I mostly just looked out the window for the duration of the trip. The German countryside was filled with a lot of hills and valleys, villages were pitched on top or on the sides of these earthworks, or else lay in the belly in between. The weather outside was cloudy, with sporadic rain and snow showers. In such an environment, it wasn't difficult to just let my mind go, and be numb to anything else going on around me. After about an hour, as the captain had said, we arrived at the front gate of the military installation that housed the Landstuhl hospital. We all presented our military IDs to the guards, and were allowed to pass through the gates into one of the entrances to the hospital. To my recollection the entrance we went to was not the front door, but more like the entrance to an emergency room of a hospital. Off to our left was what appeared to be a nurses station, with a few personnel behind or around it in discussion. The rear detachment commander took the initiative to get us where we needed to go by interrupting their conversation.

"Excuse me, could you tell us where PFC Gaunky's room is?" The conversation stopped immediately, a couple of the personnel looking a bit confused or perplexed. One or two looked as though they had not heard him clearly, and vocalized as much.

"I'm sorry, could you say that again?"

"Could you tell us where we could find PFC Gaunky's room," and with a quick pause, he raised his arm to point at me before continuing, "His brother is here to see him."

One of the personnel, a middle-aged woman, came over, a solemn and sad look on her face. "You don't know, do you?" She really didn't need to say much more for me to get the message. However, we moved, just her and me, to a back room, where she came out and told me point blank that Alex had passed on the day before. She then gave, what I can only presume to be, a sympathetic hug, thinking that I would need it. Sadly, I didn't. I forced a single tear to come out, just so that the hug would not seem worthless. At least, that is what I hope I was able to convey anyway. After a minute or so, we came back out to the nurses station. There, likely brought out while I was in the back, was a bag full of an assortment of items, and a quilt.

The nurses pointed to the bag. "These were your brother's personal effects." I took a few minutes to look through the bag. In it was a watch, a digital camera, a set of his dog tags, a photo album that contained several cards from kids to a soldier. Also in the bag was a medal box, inside of which was the medal, ribbon, and lapel pin for the Purple Heart he had been awarded. I put everything back into the bag. I then looked over to the quilt. I found it difficult for that to have been a part of Alex's personal effects. The nurse that was standing by must have surmised this, as she began to give me an explanation as to why it was there.

"This is a quilt that was put together by members of the staff of the hospital. We give one to every servicemember or family member of that servicemember that passes through here." I knew right after hearing that, exactly where that quilt was going when I got it back home. It was going to go straight to Mom. It was at this point that I remembered what I had been told by Mom and Dad before flying out to Germany over a day ago, and realized that the likelihood that they'd arrived at the hospital by this point was probably fairly low, given the speed at which events had taken place. I was here, alone. As I was about to contemplate this reality fully, I was broken out of my reverie by the sound of the nurse talking again.

The night before Alex left for his first deployment. Alex, left, in his newly issued Army Combat Uniform (ACU) and the author in his Desert Camouflage Uniform (DCU); see page xv. (*Author*)

"One of his teammates is here if you want to talk to him."

"Yes," I said, without thinking, without any hesitation at all. Remembering the SIGACT, I knew that others had been injured in the incident. Visiting with someone who was there might give me some answers, or at least an understanding of what happened. At least, that was the quick thought that ran through my head. We walked a way through the hospital until we finally reached the room the soldier was in. The soldier was the driver of Alex's vehicle, as I was to find out. And he looked in bad shape. There were some bandages on his head, presumably from the vehicle turning over multiple times, or perhaps, from landing on the ground in the aftermath. Either way, it was a significant head wound. What got me more were the bandages around his abdomen. He had been bandaged up heavily across his stomach and chest. It bothered me that he was in bad shape like this. Tubes were also stuck into or attached to him to monitor all his vitals. In spite of all these things, the driver, Private First Class Robert Van Antwerp, was responsive and coherent. He was also in mourning. This was demonstrated to me not long after we entered his room.

"Robert, someone is here to see you. This is Sergeant Gaunky." Immediately upon hearing my name, Private Van Antwerp became very sad.

"I'm sorry. I'm so, so sorry." He repeated this several times. There was guilt there, unnecessary guilt from my opinion, but then I was feeling that same guilt.

"It's okay," I replied, trying to at least assuage some of the guilt, even if for only that moment. Whether I did, or added more guilt to him, I don't know. I have hoped ever since that it was the former.

We talked for a few more minutes after this, me asking if he remembered anything, him telling me he just remembered seeing something white and then blacking out. I told him to get better, and that I'd keep him in my thoughts and prayers. We then parted, and I returned to the nurses station.

After a few minutes, with all of Alex's effects and the quilt in hand, and after having reconnected with the rear detachment commander, I left the hospital proper and moved into a room located at one of the Fisher House buildings. I had never heard of the organization before, but after my experience there, which we'll get to shortly, I'll never forget about them. Fisher House can best be summed up as similar to a Ronald McDonald House or another kind of charitable facility that provides living accommodations to the families of those receiving medical treatment at a hospital. Fisher House facilities fill that role at military posts or VA campuses. The rear detachment commander, after ensuring I was okay in the room I had been provided, gave me one more quick piece of information.

"Here is my number," he said, providing me with an office number to call if I needed to. "I'm going to call on you every other day to see how you're doing and to see if there is anything you need or that needs to get completed. If you need to get a hold of me beforehand, though, use that number." I nodded my understanding to him.

"Alright, I'm going to get headed back to the unit now. I'll get a hold of you in a couple days to see how things are going." Again, I nodded. We shook hands, and then he and his driver left. I sat for several minutes alone in the room, still on autopilot, even though I'd had a few blips of mental movement in the last few hours. I sat on the bed of a sparsely decorated room, looking outside at the cloudy sky, not a thing going on in my head.

After staring out the window in silence for somewhere between twenty and thirty minutes, a knock came at the door to the room. I got up and walked over to the door, opening it up a little in order to see who knocked, as the only person I knew at that point who knew that I was here was the rear detachment commander who had left less than an hour before. Had he forgotten something, I thought. Yet when I looked on the other side of the door, it was not the captain I had met, but instead another officer. Dressed in woodland camouflage battle dress uniform (BDUs), a wisp of white-grey hair crowning his balding head. On one lapel was an eagle, signifying him as a colonel, or what we in the army often referred to as a "full bird" in order to differentiate them from the lieutenant colonels that soldiers are more often inundated with across their careers. On his other lapel was a cross, signifying that he was a member of the chaplain's corps, in this case a Christian. Already? Did the hospital have that much concern for me, I thought.

"Sergeant Gaunky?" he asked.

"Yes Sir?"

"I'm the installation chaplain," he started, letting me know something I would have likely deduced on my own, before he continued, "Your mother called me to ask that I check up on you."

"Ah," I replied, not sure if I rolled my eyes or not, as I was and am still at times prone to do. I followed up with another quick phrased reply, "Okay."

We stood there and talked for several more minutes, and he informed me that there was work going on behind the scenes to try to help get me home for my brother's funeral. How that was going to be accomplished was not yet determined, but discussions and movements were in the works in order to figure it out. He then told me that he would visit me again in the coming days to keep an eye on me as well as keep me up to date on how I would be getting home.

After finishing our conversation, we parted, and I went back to staring out the window in silence. This lasted for about another half hour or so before I made a concerted effort to get up, and wander around the building to get an understanding of what was here for me to use, or at least help take my mind off of things I couldn't control or know at that point in time. My first stop after leaving the room was the foyer of the building, where I had crossed quickly through only hours before that morning. Once there, I rotated to take in the layout of the

The Fisher House at the Landstuhl, Germany, Regional Medical Center. (*Fisher House Foundation*)

building and get my bearings. From the foyer, into the middle of the building, was a sizable kitchen/dining area for those staying at the Fisher House. The size allowed for multiple people to cook and/or sit and eat meals as entire families, or perhaps even all occupants of the building if they so wished. Looking back through the front door of the foyer, I turned my head left. There, partly hidden by the adjoining wall, was a large sitting area with several bookcases full of reading material for the occupants as well as a single, solitary computer with internet access. My guess would be that Wi-Fi access within the house made having more than a single computer unnecessary, but for me, having come directly from a war zone without a computer of my own, it would be, by and large, my primary means of communicating with the outside world over the coming days.

A few more minutes went by as I looked around the main common areas of the Fisher House when a soldier, a non-commissioned officer like myself, came walking up to me. He was wearing, like the chaplain earlier, a woodland camouflage BDU uniform. Where he differed from the chaplain, besides his rank, was that he had two shoulder patches indicating that he was not part of the installation personnel. His unit patches, one designating his current unit, the other signifying a unit he had gone to war with, were the same. This soldier coming up to me was a member of a fairly prestigious unit in the history of the army. I would know, as I was once part of that same sizable unit. He was a member of the 101st Airborne Division (Air Assault). I continued to take in more information as he made his way towards me, wondering if he was going to simply ask, perhaps, where the men's room was in the building. I was soon to be proven wrong.

"Sergeant Gaunky?"

"Yes?" I replied, somewhat uncertainly.

"I'm Sergeant (First Class) McShan, a liaison from the 101st. I was informed that you had arrived here to see your brother."

"Yes," was the only thing I could reply. There was a few seconds silence before we talked a little more about how my flight had been from Kuwait, and then he handed me a booklet of cards, similar to the ones found in Alex's personal effects bag. There were four pictures, each slightly different from the other, which were, from the best I could tell, taken sequentially at the point where Alex received the Purple Heart. A colonel could be seen in three of the four pictures, slowly laying down the medal, while in one he was holding the certificate that normally accompanies the medal. I could see a little bit in the pictures of what had happened to Alex. Most of his head was bandaged up. There were tubes sticking out from underneath the sheets which covered up the rest of his body. They were both difficult, and not difficult, to view. I would view these pictures more in depth later, but at the time, I breezed through them and continued talking with the liaison soldier. It was at this point, that an unexpected topic came up.

"Private Van Antwerp's father is going to be here tomorrow if you want time to speak with him."

"I see," was my immediate reply, followed by, "I'll have to think about that."

"You'll have till tomorrow, so don't rush a decision right now."

"I understand." We finished talking for another minute or two, with him handing me his card to keep in contact while I was at Landstuhl, and then parted ways. For those of you wondering, Private Van Antwerp's father was, at that time, a lieutenant general in the U.S. Army, holding the position of Commander, U.S. Army Accessions Command. Put simply, he was somewhat of a big player, and one of his sons, of several in the military from what I could tell, was now injured. Understandably, he made a decision to come see his son while that son was receiving treatment for his injuries. One would think that a decision to talk to Private Van Antwerp's father would be a difficult one. It wasn't. I just needed the time to formulate my response in the best way possible when asked again.

I went back to my room in the building, lay down on the bed, and just looked out the window for what seemed like a few minutes, when in reality it was hours. By the time I left the room again, the sun was beginning to set. I walked back to the common rooms, and went into the kitchen/dining area. There I found what I was to learn were volunteers bringing in food for the people occupying the building that day. As it would turn out, there would be volunteers every day there during my stay due to it being close to Thanksgiving, though my mind was busy with other things and I forgot about that fact. I grabbed a few things to eat and found a place to sit down near an older couple who were also utilizing the Fisher House facility. The gentleman was an elderly vet, probably Korean War era, perhaps even late World War II. He was at Landstuhl to get some kind of surgery, and his wife came with him to be at his side. We briefly talked while eating our meal. They never asked, so far as I can recall, what I was doing there, and I never commented on the matter.

After dinner, I went over to the computer, followed the log on instructions, and then got onto my AKO account. I sent out several emails that evening. One, with multiple recipients on it, was to let family know that I had made it to the hospital. A few others were sent to my leadership back in Iraq to let them know, 1) that I had made it to Landstuhl, and 2) my little brother had not made it. Finishing up the emails, I went back to my room, stared outside a little longer, and then drifted off into sleep, my body exhausted, at least emotionally, from all the information it had taken in and had to process of that day's events.

20 November 2005
The next morning began with an early wake-up. It took a few minutes for me to remember that I was not still in Iraq, but in Germany, as well as for the reasons why. As early as it was, I was

slow to move. There wasn't much, at that point anyway, for me to do or anywhere to go. After showering and shaving, I went out to the kitchen/dining area to see if there was anything worth eating, largely because I knew I needed to eat. Not that I wanted to eat, but I knew I needed something to give me energy for the day. I don't recall finding anything that looked appealing, so I went to the sitting room, and looked around. Every once in awhile I would watch people move around and do what I had attempted to—get breakfast. I just remained sitting, watching, keeping silent. At some point, I picked up a book from one of the bookshelves and tried to read it, trying to keep myself occupied somehow.

Somewhere around mid-morning, Sergeant First Class McShan came into the building. I stood up as he walked over to me, and when he was close enough, we shook hands.

"Morning, Sergeant Gaunky."

"Morning," I replied back.

"So, remember what I told you yesterday about General Van Antwerp coming in today. Well, he's here now. If you want to talk with him, now's the time to say something."

I took a few minutes to remember the answer I had come to the previous evening, before finally replying, "I thank you and him for the invitation, but I'm going to pass on this one."

"Are you sure?" McShan asked, clearly wanting me to consider his request carefully.

"Yes, I'm sure. Besides, I think it'd be more beneficial for him to spend as much time as he can with his son," I replied, the images of seeing Private Van Antwerp coming back to the forefront of my mind. We talked a few minutes more, and then parted ways. I would not see him again at Fisher House.

Most of the rest of the day seems like a blur, but there were three things within that blur that stand out to me, even this many years removed. The first was some kind of thought in my head that I needed to get, at bare minimum, parts for a dress uniform. I couldn't tell you why such thoughts came into my head, but they did, and I called the rear detachment commander to see if we could go to the nearest military clothing and sales to pick up those parts, and if possible, get a rush job done to get it sufficiently altered before I ended up flying back home. The second thing I remember was, at some point in the afternoon, writing a poem in honor of Alex. Like the sudden urge to get parts for a dress uniform, this too came out of the blue, but also felt necessary. I would write it in an email that I sent off to family after I felt the words conveyed what I felt they needed to say. Because this was at a time when MySpace was really just starting to make waves, and Facebook wasn't quite on the map yet, the only real way for family to see and share this if they so chose to view it was through email. I entitled it "Bravest of the Brave." It was very much a stream of thought type of piece, and went as follows:

> *Bravest of the Brave*
> *Truest of the true*
> *My brother could give a smile*
> *To anyone he knew*
> *Bravest of the Brave*
> *Freest of the free*
> *My brother gave his whole heart*
> *In all that he believed*
> *Bravest of the brave*

Heart of all our hearts
My brother knew that in ours
His love would never part
Tear upon all tears
And bravest of the brave
He knows that when tears fall
We will always hear his name
In the early morning dawn
As our tears fall down like rain
We will always know my brother
As the bravest of the brave

The last thing that stands out from that second day was a conversation I had with a volunteer at the facility around dinner time. Like the day before, the volunteers brought in significant quantities of food. As I began filling my plate, I passed by a volunteer in civilian clothes, but with the tell-tale "high and tight" haircut of a military servicemember. After looking around and getting more to put on my plate, I said to the individual, "Man, this is a lot of food. And a lot of people to bring it to boot."

"Yeah," he started. "It's Thanksgiving time, so we always make sure to bring in something for the people who pass through here."

"Always?"

"Oh yeah. We rotate units to help support this place on holidays. I've been doing it for at least a few years now."

"Wow. That's definitely a lot of support." From there, we meandered on to an otherwise casual discussion, with me stating that I was one of the people staying there when he asked. The reason I gave him was that I was there because of a family member, though I didn't get much more into the details of the situation. After our short conversation, I went back into the sitting room, finished whatever food I had on my plate, and then eventually went back to my room to get some more sleep, not entirely sure what the next day would hold for me.

21 November 2005

The next day didn't move quite as slowly as the previous one. I was planning to make a trip off of the hospital campus with the rear detachment commander to go to another military post where a military clothing and sales store was located. This became even more important when I learned from the installation chaplain early that morning that there was now a definitive plan on how to get me home. That plan was to make me a "Special Escort" for Alex's remains, which would start in two days, Wednesday, the 23rd. He told me we would meet later that afternoon to go to the hospital to talk to the medical examiner from the mortuary affairs department and have a quick discussion about the plan. As such, it became imperative that I get an army dress uniform, or at least parts for it.

The rear detachment commander and I left the hospital complex around 9 a.m. that morning and drove for forty-five minutes or so to the closest post with a military clothing and sales store. Once there, I spent around a half hour looking for all the components necessary for making up a complete "Class A" dress military uniform, from dress uniform rank, shoes, belt, other patches, awards, etc., to coat and trousers. The salesperson working that day came to me a couple times to ask if I needed any help. She was, from all I could tell, a spouse of a soldier serving in Germany. One recommendation she made after I explained that I needed parts for a Class A uniform, was that I should go with the Marlow White line, as that line was much more professional looking, and made of better looking, for that matter, material. After taking her suggestion to heart, and getting a set of trousers and coat, and allowing for comparatively quick altering, I went to collect more materials for the uniform. Unfortunately, they lacked the sergeant's rank for the uniform, which struck me as odd that they would be out; I also found that they didn't have the distinctive unit insignia (DUI) for my unit based in Hawaii, though that made sense seeing as they were a store in Germany serving those units stationed there. I made a note of the two missing items, and reminded myself to get a hold of my unit leadership back in Iraq to see how this problem could be addressed.

Just prior to going to the cash register to pay for the uniform, I went over to the salesperson, with a quick question that just occurred to me regarding getting the uniform altered. "Excuse me, ma'am, how quickly could I get the trousers and coat altered, including getting some of these patches sewn on?"

She took a couple minutes of thought and then responded, "Earliest we could get it done is Friday."

"You couldn't get it done any earlier?"

"Sorry, no," she replied. Knowing that it meant it couldn't be done before I left for home, I simply went to the register, and paid for all of the pieces, including a plastic garment bag. The rear detachment commander and I then left and returned to Landstuhl, arriving back a little after 1 p.m.

Around 3 p.m., the chaplain once again came to Fisher House. I met him out in the main sitting room. We walked over to the main hospital, and then proceeded to traverse many corridors and hallways until we reached our destination. There we met a middle-aged man, with a slightly overweight frame, glasses, and a balding head, not unlike that of the chaplain. We were introduced, and then moved into a small room, reminiscent of a funeral home, ironically enough.

"There he is," the man said, and pointed to an open casket.

Before moving over to see what I knew I had previously hoped never to encounter this young, I turned to the mortuary affairs specialist.

"Two quick things before I look, if that is okay."

"Of course."

"Well, first, can I get a copy of the preliminary autopsy that was done on him?" I was somewhat hesitant at this request, not sure if it would even be given a passing thought. What came back surprised me.

"Shouldn't be a problem. It'll take me a few minutes to make a copy, but we should be able to get you a copy before you leave today."

"Thanks," I replied, before asking my second request. "Is it possible I can get a copy of the initial death certificate as well? I have a feeling we're going to need it when I get home."

"Yes, I think we can do that. I'll put it in with the preliminary autopsy report."

"Thanks," I replied.

"Well, I'm going to give you a few moments alone while I get those reports copied. If you need anything, give the nurses station outside a holler," and then he stepped outside.

I took my time making it over to the coffin. I was hesitant, probably not unlike so many others approaching a loved one. When I finally got there, I spent several minutes just taking everything in. The swelling around his head and neck made it seem like the military had gotten it wrong. That it couldn't be Alex at all. It took me a few minutes to find the features that told me that this was indeed Alex. The uniform he had was a bit off. He was missing the flash behind his Air Assault wings. The distinctive unit insignias were missing on his epaulets above his shoulders and on his beret. All too quickly I knew that these would need to be corrected, and thanked God that Alex had left a dress uniform at home in Wisconsin with these things on them, so that I could correct this wrong. For whatever reason, I didn't even think to let the people at the hospital or the mortuary affairs unit know they missed a couple of details. Why, when I could just as quickly correct them myself when I got home? Even after taking several minutes to look at uniform corrections, and just as many trying to find Alex amidst the swelling from his head and neck injuries, I still couldn't quite believe it was him. It was then that I slowly took my right hand, and carefully put it down on his chest, to see if I could feel the up and down motion of him breathing, and thus perhaps find this to be a bad joke. I also hoped I'd find that perhaps underneath the uniform, if I put enough pressure with my hand, I'd find that instead of a body, it was more of a doll or model, similar to those found at clothing stores in a mall. No breathing came. Neither did the sensation that this was a doll. It was real. The whole situation was real. This loss was real. There was no denying it now. For a few more minutes, I stood in silence, just me, Alex, and the coffin. Then both the mortuary affairs specialist and chaplain returned.

"Here are those documents," he said as he handed them to me in a folder. I shook his hand, and thanked him, but couldn't look him in the eye. I turned back to the chaplain.

"We're going to meet over at the mortuary affairs building tomorrow, 1100 hours for your briefing and instructions. I'll come get you at Fisher House so we can walk over there together." I nodded my understanding. I was then dismissed. I found my way over to the little shoppette on post and grabbed a sub sandwich to eat. I forced it down. There was nothing else to do at that point, so I slowly wandered back to the Fisher House, where I wrote two emails. One was to my family letting them know that I was apparently going to be Alex's escort for the journey home (some already knew, as it had been the casualty assistance officers consulting with them who had initiated the process of getting me assigned that duty), and that I was expected to head out sometime on Wednesday. The second email was to my leadership back in Iraq, letting them know that I needed, at the least, my distinctive unit insignia as well as a unit patch from my outfit back in Hawaii to complete my dress uniform when I got home. Those two emails sent, I went back to my room, and looked outside the window into the grey, cloud covered, and cold day until I passed out. It had been a long, long day.

22 November 2005

Like every morning the last few days, this one passed by both
slowly and quickly. Today, though, I had specific activities to
attend to or accomplish. One I knew about, a mission briefing
just before lunch, the other I would find out a little bit later as
I walked to the official mortuary affairs building for my briefing.
The chaplain met me in the lobby of the Fisher House at
around a quarter after ten that morning. We then walked across
the military compound to the opposite side of the hospital to a
building that was set apart from the medical facilities. While on
the way, the chaplain let me know that Alex's vehicle leader was
at the facility, and that he would be coming out of some kind of
surgery to deal with an injury from the incident. He told me
that if I wanted to meet the individual I could go to his hospital
room afterwards. I told him that I would like that, and so he
gave me the room number, and the approximate time frame
when Alex's team leader would be able to be seen. As he
finished, we finally approached our intended destination.

Like most buildings in the military, it had a placard in front
of it designating the building number, as well as the office or
function inside. This building, old with a brick casing, was
strictly for the purposes of autopsy and mortuary affairs. It was
a building meant to take care of the dead, more so than the
living who worked in it. We walked in, and were guided to a
decent-sized conference room. I sat on one side of a table,
having been directed to it, with a window on the opposite side
of the room beaming a dull light onto its surface. In front of me
was a baby blue pocket envelope, similar to what students may
use in class to hold their papers and notes. It lay closed, and I
decided to not open it until I was told.

Into the conference room walked two individuals, one a junior enlisted soldier, a specialist, and the other a senior enlisted soldier. I stood up.

"Morning," the non-commissioned officer, Master Sergeant Brown, said as he walked in. "Take a seat." We all did as he instructed, even the chaplain.

Master Sergeant Brown looks at me, before saying, "You must be Sergeant Gaunky."

"Yes, master sergeant," I replied.

"Before we get started, I just want to say, you and your family have my most sincere condolences."

"Thank you," I said, which was followed by a moment or so of uncomfortable silence.

"Alright," he started, breaking the silence, "go ahead and open the folder in front of you." I did so, and saw groups of papers on both sides, some being sets of orders, others being official forms I'd probably have to fill out, and then there was an itinerary for plane tickets.

"This is your official briefing for a special escort duty. If you could please take out the first set of papers on the right side of your folder." I did so, and he continued. "The following are your instructions for your temporary duty (referred to in army parlance as TDY) as a special escort for the remains of Private First Class Gaunky." He let that sink in for a moment, and then once again continued. "As you can see, you will meet up with the specialist here," he pointed to the other soldier in the room, "at four o'clock a.m. at the Fisher House entrance to come over to the mortuary affairs building. You will be in Class A (dress) uniform."

"Um," I interrupted him, "I don't have a Class A uniform."

"You don't have a dress uniform?" he repeated, in somewhat of a cautious manner.

"Not a full one, I have pieces that I picked up the other day, but no full, complete, uniform. I just came out of a combat zone." There was a moment of silence while that sentiment just floated in the air. Finally, Master Sergeant Brown spoke.

"You should have let us know, we could have gotten you one." He didn't say it in any kind of angry way, but there was a noticeable level of disbelief, possibly frustration, but there wasn't a whole lot that could have been done differently unless everyone would have known this would have happened.

"Well, wear the best clothes you have, and be professional to the extent you can given your circumstances." He spent another half hour or so going over the instructions about rendering honors whenever the casket was put into or taken out of its mode of transportation, the paperwork that needed to be completed, etc. Before we completed the portion about the paperwork for the mission, Master Sergeant Brown made the following commentary in order to impress upon me how important it was to follow through with the responsibilities of this assignment. "I know that he's your brother, and that you're going to be a little bit distracted, but it is important that things get done by the book. It is important that the paperwork gets done. Don't forget that." He spent a few more minutes talking about the rest of the responsibilities, as well as the fact that the orders covered a five day period. As such, once I had turned the remains over to their next of kin, my Dad, I went from being the military escort of said remains to one of just several military representatives to the family. After this, he concluded the formal presentation of the briefing.

"Do you have any questions?"

"Yes," I started, "is the coffin and packaging surrounding it already set up?" Why I asked this question I'm not entirely sure. Maybe I wanted to make sure things were prepared enough so that we weren't having to do last minute preparations that might impact being on time for all of our responsibilities. Maybe I did it for some other reason that remains hidden in my subconscious. Regardless, I asked it.

"Oh, everything is already ready. The coffin and its packaging is complete, and in the hearse already."

"Okay, good," I replied. "Well, I guess that's all I have." We all stood up, and Master Sergeant Brown once again offered me his condolences and then shook my hand. I shook the hand of the other soldier that I'd met in the morning, and shook hands with the chaplain. It was the last time I would see him during this stay on Landstuhl. I walked out of the building, looked at the time, and ended up going to the shoppette to get something to eat for lunch.

Some time after 3 p.m., I went back to the hospital and went to the room number the chaplain had given me for the other soldier in Alex's unit who had in the last few days been transported here for treatment. I walked into the room, and looked first to my left, then to my right. Only one person was in the room, and he was off to my right. While walking over toward him, I took in what I could of his injuries. It looked as if one of his legs had been elevated slightly, and a cast had been placed on one of his arms. Beyond that, he didn't look too worse for wear.

"Sergeant Prater?" I inquired.

"Yeah?" he replied, uncertain likely who I was at that point, much less why I was in his hospital room.

"I'm Sergeant Gaunky, Alex's older brother."

"Oh, man, I'm so sorry," was his immediate reply.

"Hey, man, it's okay," I replied, trying, as I had with Private Van Antwerp, to assuage any feelings of guilt he may have had. We then talked for a few minutes, me asking him some questions like I had Private Van Antwerp to see if he remembered anything, and telling him I wished him a full and speedy recovery. For his part, Sergeant Prater told me roughly the same thing as Van Antwerp, that he saw something white and then blacked out. We parted ways as best as we could under such a situation, both trying to process what it was we were respectively having to endure from the situation.

I left his room and slowly made my way back to the Fisher House facility. Before heading back to my room, I went to the administrative office in the building to see what the charges were going to be for the few phone calls I'd made back to the states, and to see how best to pay for them. When I got there, there was a woman, probably not more than a few years older than I was, working at a desk. I mentioned my room number, said that I'd made some calls back to the states on the phone in the room, and asked if there would be anyone there when I left in the early morning hours the next day for me to pay for the charges. She said that there wouldn't be, but that things should be okay as long as the calls were made on my phone card. Fisher House, apparently, gives out phone cards to those who are receiving lodging there, but I hadn't gotten one when I arrived or any day since. I told her as much.

"You didn't get a card when you came in?" was her immediate reply, followed with a somewhat nervous chuckle, in realizing that such an oversight rarely happens at the facility. My guess would be that it was because my check-in had either been done over the phone before I'd arrived through the rear detachment commander, or he had gotten a card and had just forgotten to give it to me. Either way, the matter was settled within ten minutes, with me paying out the costs, thanking the individual for her understanding and help, and then returning to my room. I stayed there, watching as the sun fell, waiting for my body to fall asleep. Before it did so, I set the alarm on the clock to wake me up with enough time to finish packing up the few little things I had out, shower, shave, and put on the clothes I would have for this rather surprising, and up until the briefing earlier that day, little heard-of mission. I passed out somewhere around eleven that evening.

THREE

Mission Escort Duty

Germany and United States
23 November 2005

The alarm on the clock went off at 3:20. I shut if off, turned on the lights, and looked out the window. It was snowing. Given the cold I'd felt the last several days, and the way the wind was blowing, it was probably even colder this morning. I took about twenty minutes to get myself ready. I finished up packing those things not immediately necessary, and then took my garment bag, my duffel bag, and the blue folder with me, exiting the room I'd spent the last five days in for the last time. All the lights in the building were off, and I had to carefully navigate the halls so as not to disturb others who were sleeping. I stayed just inside the front entrance for a while, watching the snow blow around in the few lights outside on the hospital compound. I then took my stuff as it got closer to 4:00, and went outside, making sure my fleece was closed tight and my watch cap covered both my ears. Four a.m. came and went. I became concerned that perhaps I'd misheard the instructions given to me the previous day. Time rolled on; 4:10. 4:20. 4:30. All I had was my few belongings, the snow, and my thoughts running through my head that I had missed something or that something had happened to keep the driver occupied. Every minute that passed, I became more and more worried. Around 4:45, a vehicle pulled up into the circular drive outside the Fisher House. I looked to see a soldier step out. It was the soldier from yesterday. My anxieties were somewhat relieved at seeing him, telling me things weren't quite as bad as my mind had been making them. What disconcerted me, however, was that the soldier was in his dress greens, his "Class A" uniform, making me more self-conscious that I wasn't dressed the same way.

"Morning," I called out to him.

"Morning," he replied. "Go ahead and jump in, we'll get to the office in a few minutes."

I did as I was instructed, fastening my seatbelt and keeping my belongings in my lap. The drive was less than five minutes, with almost no traffic to speak of in the early morning hours of the day. We approached an entrance I was not familiar with, for which the soldier touched a garage door opener attached to his car visor, and a door opened. He pulled his vehicle in, and we stepped out, then walked through the building to another garage, where a hearse was parked. I went to the back door on the passenger's side, and carefully placed my duffel and garment bag right behind the passenger's seat. I noticed in the back there was a long, white container kept tightly in place by cords and straps. On it was documentation and a scanning strip, similar to what mail carriers use when transporting larger packages. I closed the door, and then heard from the soldier to go ahead and jump into the passenger seat, which I did. He stepped into the driver's seat, pressed another garage opener, pulled out, closed the garage door behind us, and then we began our drive, the first part of the escort mission, from the hospital over to Frankfurt International Airport. I would begin the second part of the escort mission by plane.

After a few moments of silence, with nothing but the wind blowing and the snow falling, I decided to start a conversation, though probably not in the smartest way.

"Are we . . . are we going to be late?" I asked, my concern about the late start impacting everything else.

"No, we'll be okay. The point of the early start was to make sure we had a buffer on time. Happens all the time," he replied. With that anxiety lessened, we started some casual conversations about sports, the weather, and other mundane subjects. At some point, I started up another odd conversation that struck me, but with nothing else to do, I just went with it.

"So, what's your MOS (military occupational specialty)?"

"Truck driver," he replied.

"Really? So how did you end up here?"

"Orders. I was in a transportation unit before this. Even did a deployment. When we got back they sent me here."

"How long now?"

"About six months," he replied.

"So how are you liking it?" realizing just after I said it that "liking" was probably the wrong term. If that offended him, he made no indication of it, and instead answered with an earnest reply.

"Actually, it's not all that bad. To be honest, it's probably one of the more fulfilling and honorable things to be doing. I consider it one of the most honorable missions I've ever done."

There was a pause, after which we went on talking as before. After a brief break in the conversation, another anxious thought came back to me, one that had been haunting me since the briefing the other day, and that had really been haunting me the whole time I was at Landstuhl. I decided to ask a question that would either amplify or help mitigate that concern.

"Has this ever happened before," I started.

"What do you mean," he asked seeking clarification.

"Someone being an escort without a dress uniform. Has anyone ever done that, particularly from a war zone?" I wanted to see how unique my situation was, so I added that last detail.

"It doesn't happen often, but yeah, you're not the first."

"Really?"

"Oh yeah. We had a major come through once, kinda similar to your situation in that he was coming from a war zone, so no dress uniform. He was intent on escorting the soldier from his unit home. An exception was made for him. So yeah, it does happen, just not a lot." His response relieved a little bit of the anxiety I'd been having. With that answer, we again went back to subjects of a casual nature for most of the rest of the drive.

A few minutes after 6:30 we started driving into an industrial area around the airport where a lot of the shipping and other such activities occur. We pulled up to a ramp, where the soldier backed up so that the rear of the hearse was facing the ramp.

"Stay here, I'll be back in a few minutes," he said, and then stepped out of the vehicle with a handful of paperwork. He went over to an office area of the building, where lights were already on, and spent several minutes in the office. When he returned, I got out of the hearse, and both he and I went to the back of the vehicle. The soldier opened the door, and then undid some of the latches and restraints, and then did something so that the package was partially pushed out from the hearse. I took that as my cue to prepare to render honors, as had been directed to me the previous day in the mission briefing. We waited about two minutes as a man on a forklift came out, and then proceeded to carefully extract the coffin in its packaging the rest of the way out of the vehicle. The soldier and I both went to attention, and then we both gave slow, solemn salutes as the coffin was removed. After the man had gotten back far enough out of our line of sight, we both slowly lowered our salutes, and watched for a few minutes as the coffin was moved into a holding area, to be prepared for the flight.

"Alright, time to get you to the departure gate," the soldier said, and we both re-entered the hearse. The drive to the gate was about fifteen minutes or so. I stepped out of the vehicle, opened the back passenger door to grab my two bags, closed it, then went back to look into the vehicle and the soldier in the driver's seat.

"Thanks," was all I said. He merely smiled. We shook hands, and then I stepped back, watching him travel off and disappear into the sunrise.

I walked into the terminal and attempted to find the check-in counter for my flight.

It took me a few minutes to find the correct line, which was quite long. Despite the early hour, there were surprisingly a lot of people in the airport. At the time, I had forgotten that it was the day before Thanksgiving, and while many Germans didn't necessarily celebrate the holiday, a lot of Americans overseas did, and were thus likely trying to catch flights home to celebrate with their families. I took my military ID card from my wallet, flight information, as well as a copy of my escort orders, and stepped up to the available agent when directed to come forward. After setting my documents and ID down on the desk, I spent a couple of minutes talking to the agent so that she understood my situation, and checked my duffel bag as well as my garment bag full of uniform pieces. The agent, a mid-thirties woman with a slight German accent, followed along and nodded her head as she listened, at the same time she was inputting my information into her computer terminal. I was then directed to the security check-in to head toward my flight gate. That line, too, was surprisingly long. I passed through that security checkpoint without issue, and then looked at a local terminal map to find my gate destination. The walk to the gate reminded me of my times at O'Hare in Chicago, where it seemed like a race to get to a connecting flight on the opposite side of the terminal. Along the way, I passed through a second security area, where I had to once again take off my shoes, belt, and place my document folder under an x-ray machine before proceeding on to my gate.

I walked for several more minutes only to find the waiting area for the gate not yet opened. I then backtracked a bit to a duty free shop I'd seen and picked up either a *Time* or *Newsweek* magazine, as those were my preferred reads on flights. I walked back to the area near the gate, and found a bench to sit on. There I sat and read, and from time to time watched as other passengers began to do the same, waiting for the gate area to open. It would be a couple of hours before it would do so. When it appeared that some of the service personnel were getting ready to open it up, a number of us got up and formed a line for the information desk as soon as it was available. There were half a dozen people in front of me when the doors opened, and a lot more behind me. Slowly, the line moved toward the desk, and when it was my turn, I presented my ID, boarding pass, and orders to the attendant. I explained, as I had at the original check-in desk when I entered the airport, the details, or at least as much as I was allowed or comfortable to say, about the responsibilities that were required of me. I was probably a little too insistent about being able to get to the ground floor when they were loading Alex's coffin, but at the time I felt I needed to be. The service personnel nodded and gave an occasional "yes" or "uh huh" in response. When I felt satisfied that the individual understood, I walked over to my right and into the official waiting area. I took a seat at the window, keeping the plane, or rather a wing of it, in my line of sight so I could make sure I followed through with the rendering of honors that was required of me, both in my orders, and as I saw it as an older brother.

Sometime within a half hour or so of staring out the window toward the plane, I turned my eyes briefly to see a soldier walk into the waiting area. He was wearing his "B" uniform, meaning no dress coat. What he did have was a black pullover sweater, with name plate and branch insignia on one side, as well as shoulder boards on his epaulets to signify his rank.

"Sergeant Gaunky?" he asked me as I got up. I nodded my head, and at the same time, I internally cursed myself. Why hadn't I thought to get a "B" uniform ready. All that would've been required was hemming up of the pants legs and getting a name plate.

We shook hands, and then he explained that he had been sent from some higher headquarters, which one I can't remember anymore, to come and support me while I waited for the plane to be loaded, boarded, and set for takeoff. We both stood, as though not sure whether or not to sit down, and talked for what seemed like an hour or so, but was probably no more than fifteen minutes, before one of the staff came to let us know that the crew were getting ready to bring Alex from the loading area to the plane, to be placed in the underbelly of the aircraft. We both nodded and were escorted out a door and down several flights of stairs until we hit the tarmac. We then walked about twenty-five to thirty feet, and saw a lift with a belt feed in place by the side of the aircraft.

When we got to the loading machine, the loading foreman shook both our hands. He stated that it would be a few more minutes before Alex arrived. We both nodded our heads. The foreman then talked with us for the time that we were waiting, stating that he had been in the service as well, though it had been years since he had been in. Finally, a lift came carrying a large container, an LD2 as it turned out. Inside the container was the packaged coffin, and in the coffin, Alex. As they put the container on the conveyor, both the soldier and I went to attention, and then saluted as the container slowly went up, and then was moved by a couple of crew members into place in the plane's underbelly. When it was officially onboard, the soldier and I slowly released our salutes, and then relaxed our postures ever so slightly. The foreman brought us back to the stairs, and escorted us back up to the gangway that led in one direction back to the waiting area, and in the other, the plane itself. As we were ascending the stairs, an announcement could be heard that first class passengers were now to line up for boarding. I was in coach, far back no less, so I figured it would just be smart for me to walk back into the waiting area with my ticket in hand. As we walked in, I was stopped by one of the personnel from the counter.

"We've upgraded your ticket," she said, before laying her hand out to take my boarding pass back. She tore it up there, then handed me the new boarding pass. First Class seating.

"You can just go ahead and board now," she said, giving off a small, sad smile, and indicating the direction to the plane.

It was hard for me to believe that I'd just gotten an upgraded ticket. As I got on, one of the flight attendants greeted me, and I walked around to find my seat, as it was labeled on the new boarding pass. I found it and sat down. And then I waited.

Over a period of several minutes, I watched as others entered the plane into the first-class section, almost certainly none of whom had been upgraded. I tried to hide myself, since I was not in any kind of business attire, formal or otherwise, but rather in a pair of overly large khakis with a short sleeved t-shirt and black fleece jacket over the top of that. I felt like I looked nothing like someone who travels first class. And yet, I just sat there, waiting. There weren't any particular looks from the other passengers of this section as they took their seats. Those passing through to coach/economy seating were a different matter. They noticed what I noticed, that there was seemingly a disconnect between my appearance and my sitting in that section. I would imagine being in uniform, full uniform, would have probably tempered the sentiment I saw in their eyes. Yet I just sat there, waiting. At some point, a flight attendant walked through, and stopped by my seating section, of which I was the only occupant.

"Can I get you anything to drink?" she asked.

"Drink?" I asked, a little startled and confused, though I probably shouldn't have been.

"Yes. Champagne, Mimosa, Bloody Mary . . ." she mentioned before I interrupted her.

"Do you have just plain orange juice?"

"Indeed we do."

"Just that, just . . . uh . . . orange juice." She nodded with a smile, noticing my discomfort. After gathering a few more drink requests, and getting those drinks, she returned to my seat, and handed me the container of orange juice. It was at that point that I told her about being a military escort for a soldier's remains, though I omitted the fact that I was the soldier's blood relative. I then told her that, if possible, I needed to be the first person off the aircraft when we landed so that I could render honors and check to see that things had traveled overseas well. She nodded her understanding, and went on about her responsibilities of bringing other passengers their drink orders. Somewhat less agitated, I took the drink of orange juice and slowly sipped it down. Just after takeoff, I dozed off into what turned out to be a three-hour nap.

When I awoke from my nap, I looked around to get a reminder of my surroundings and responsibilities. With nowhere to go while we were in flight, I pulled out the periodical I had been reading earlier to either re-read articles I'd already read, complete ones I had yet to finish, or read ones I had yet to get to. After another hour or so passed, I found myself feeling the need to remind the crew, for whatever reason, that I wanted to be the first person off the plane when it landed, and the reason why. I got a hold of a flight attendant, stated who I was, probably again to the same flight attendant from before, and that I needed to be able to get off as soon as possible after we landed in order to perform the tasks I was required to complete. The flight attendant assured me that she understood, and that she would make sure the captain and first officer were aware. After she walked away, I went back to reading, the only thing I could do to distract myself from the mix of mission focus, and concern I had in making sure I did this thing right.

Around 3:00 p.m., eastern time, our aircraft hit the tarmac of the international airport in Cincinnati, Ohio. As we began to taxi over to our arrival gate, the captain welcomed us to the city, and to the United States, as all captains are seemingly impressed upon to do. After giving us a quick time and weather update, the captain began to talk about how they had been carrying the remains of a soldier, a fallen hero, on board, and then he asked the passengers to please wait for that soldier's escort, me, to leave the plane before they themselves did so. I was quickly motioned over to one of the doors by the flight attendant, with some looks at me as I left my seat. I quickly, though safely, made it to the door of the plane, and waited there with the flight attendant as we waited for the gate gangway to extend over the door. After a loud clicking sound, the crew member opened the door, and ushered me out. I was met by a couple of individuals on the other side of the door. One was in the familiar attire of a ground crewman, most likely the foreman for the crew helping out this flight. The other was a woman in a reddish business coat. After identifying herself as a member of either the airline or the airport senior staff, we went to the closest exit that would allow us to head down to the tarmac. It was cold when we exited. No snow was falling, but the sky had a grey cloudy tinge to it, as though it could start snowing at any point. We walked for several minutes out to the side of the aircraft, where a mobile conveyor was already getting into place. Less than a minute later, the LD2 unit was slowly removed from the plane. I went to attention, and saluted, as the cargo container was brought fully down and put onto a loader. I released my salute, went over to quickly check on the container, and was then escorted by the woman in the reddish coat back into the inside of the airport.

Alex's first encounter with U.S. soil upon his return from war had been with a couple ground crew members, a local airport/airline senior executive, and me. I was the only military representative to watch as Alex arrived home. There was no "dignified transfer," in which a crew of several servicemembers from that individual's branch carefully off-loaded the body from a military aircraft. No waiting dignitaries such as the president, vice president, secretary of defense, or congressperson. No cameras of the press, demanding to see the flag-draped coffin. We weren't even in Dover, Delaware, where most such things occur. We had bypassed it completely; the non-ceremony, though done with a ceremonial touch, could never replace what should have been done. By all kinds of metrics, we did what is said to never happen when a fallen soldier returns home.

After entering the airport's interior, I was escorted off to the side of the traditional customs area. No forms were required of me to fill out at this point, just a copy of my orders. I was taken to a closed-off area, where I met a member of the Transportation Security Agency, the TSA, who had a chair, a metallic wand, and a plastic container in the vicinity. I was asked to remove all contents of my pockets, take off my shoes, and extend my arms out parallel to the floor. I did these things, which took a few minutes to do despite my not having all that much with me. The security guard began to wand me in order to meet the basic security protocols to ensure I was not a threat. Knowing, somehow, that I was a military remains escort, the guard at one point during the wanding said, "You know, it's probably a good thing you aren't in uniform. That's a whole lot of metal." I laughed a little bit, agreeing with the guard completely. She then told me to turn around, wanded my back, and then, when she was finished, told me I could take all of my items back. A few minutes later, shoes back on, items where they needed to be, I was directed out the other side of the security enclosure, where I was once again met by the woman in the reddish coat. She escorted me to what was a lounge or club-like facility.

"This is where you'll stay until your flight is ready. Someone will come get you when things get closer." I merely nodded my understanding, and the woman left. I stayed in that lounge facility for over two hours, leaving only twice, once to utilize a restroom, the second to go over to the local book/newspaper vendor in order to get something to read and keep my mind occupied. Later, I was met by a different representative. She came up to me, shook my hand, and then we walked over to the gate area for the flight I was supposed to be on. Instead of staying in the waiting area, however, we immediately descended down to the tarmac. A loader driven by a member of the ground crew was coming over carrying a large, white cardboard packaged box. I knew what it was immediately, as I had seen it many hours ago, before it had been placed into a containerized box for shipping back from Germany. Alex had once again arrived. I went to attention as the box was put onto the conveyor that had not more than a few minutes before removed luggage from the last flight this plane had been used for. I raised my arm, again, into the all too familiar salute as Alex was lifted up once again into the belly of another aircraft, this time without the extra protection.

Once Alex was inside, I lowered my salute, and tempered my stance. The representative and I walked back up the stairs to the gangway, where I was told to just go ahead and get onto the flight. I did so, only to find that the crew was finishing up cleaning from the last flight and the new crew was coming on to set up for the next one for which I was to be a part. I found my seat, coach section this time, as my original ticket had been for the last one, though thankfully, I was not as far back on this flight as I was originally supposed to have been on the last. I found my seat, either a middle or window seat, and sat down, reading a little more as the crew made final cleaning sweeps and changeover instructions around me. After what seemed like twenty minutes, though was probably no more than ten, people began to file into the aircraft for the flight. I moved to let people into their seats, and read. I made sure, as with the last flight, that the crew knew about my escort responsibilities, and then just waited for us to take off. This flight, unlike the last, wasn't long enough for me to get a nap, at just a little over an hour, so I merely took to reading and, where possible, looking out the window to see what I could.

We touched down in Milwaukee somewhere between 7:30 and 8:00 p.m. The captain announced that they had been carrying the remains of a fallen soldier on board, and that passengers were asked to wait until after the soldier's escort exited the plane before they did so as well. Very similar to the last flight in that regard. I left the plane, and was led down to the tarmac once again. When I got there, things were different than they had been in Cincinnati. There was a hearse parked near the plane. Nearby, a large van or sport utility vehicle could be seen, as well as the flashing lights of a police vehicle. I walked over to where they were, not far from an incoming offload conveyor, and found several soldiers, all clad in Class A uniforms, with polished jump boots in place of the normal dress shoes. The first person I met was a Chief Warrant Officer 2 (CW2), who was the head of this element of soldiers. Despite my not being in uniform, and I was reminded again of this by the sight of theirs, which brought back a level of discomfort I had not felt since Germany, I saluted the officer. Next to him was a staff sergeant, the Non-commissioned Officer in Charge (NCOIC) of the element. We briefly shook hands as they both said, in acknowledgment of who I was, "Sergeant Gaunky."

"Sir, staff sergeant," I replied, looking at each in turn as I did so.

"We're the honor guard team. We came from Fort Campbell," the staff sergeant stated, probably seeing a bit of the confusion in my eyes and wanting to alleviate it. I merely nodded my head in understanding.

"Do you have the flag?" he then asked.

"Flag?" I responded, a bit confused.

"The flag for the coffin."

"Oh," I said, remembering the details given to me in my briefing now over a day before. "It's inside the coffin."

"You don't have access to it?"

"No," I replied, suddenly aware of how quickly things had just gone downhill, or at least seemingly appeared to be so.

"Ah, okay. Soldier," the staff sergeant turned his head to another soldier within the detail, continuing with, "go grab the flag from the vehicle." I was clearly taken aback and shaken at this. Had I screwed up this part of the mission that badly? My next thought was, why did they have a flag handy? Do such elements always have an extra around in case an escort doesn't have access to the one they normally—out of Dover at least—were supposed to be carrying? The staff sergeant clearly saw the look on my face, which brought about a small, sad smile on his face before he explained.

"Your parents are divorced, so we have an extra flag to give to the other parent." I nodded, somewhat relieved, but not fully.

We then turned our attention back to the plane as the casket, and Alex, were finally being extricated from the underbelly. The packaging was still on, including banding wrap to ensure that it didn't come off accidentally while in transit. Several of the soldiers came up around the conveyor while the soldier who had gotten the flag and the staff sergeant physically got onto the conveyor machine while the casket was partially out of the plane. The warrant officer and I went to attention, and presented a salute as we watched the two soldiers remove the banding and packaging off of the casket, and then carefully and safely put the flag they had taken out of their vehicle over it. The conveyor went in reverse a little bit once everything was ready and the two soldiers were off of the machine. It then lowered the casket, with six soldiers surrounding it. As the casket became parallel with the ground, the soldiers took the handles for the pallbearers and carefully carried it the last few feet until the only thing supporting the casket was this team of soldiers. The hearse backed up so that the distance between the aircraft and the plane was minimized. The soldiers placed, in a slow methodical manner, the flag-draped casket into the back of the hearse. A member of the funeral home to which the vehicle belonged, left the driver's side of the vehicle to help make sure the casket was securely in place in the back. The whole time, beyond watching this all transpire, I did nothing but keep up my salute. It was all I could do at this point, as my job was not considered complete until the end of the funeral, where I was to remain, still a member of the military's representation to the family. Finally, after the casket was secure, and the back of the hearse closed, I released my salute. Not long after this, a member of the flight crew brought me my two pieces of luggage, the garment bag being taped up as though it had been cut open during one of the flights. I thanked them and the soldiers, as the representative from the funeral home came over.

"Hi, my name is Jeff. I'm from the Lanham-Miller (later to be renamed Lanham-Schanhofer) Funeral Home. You'll be riding with me, unless you want to go with the honor guard."

"No, that's okay," I replied. I took my bags, and went to the passenger side door.

"Go ahead, it's open."

I nodded in reply, and opened the door, took my seat, and placed the bags down on my legs just above the floor. Jeff got into the driver's side.

"There's a soda and a bag of pretzels on the dashboard if you're hungry," he said. I took the items from the dash, placed the can of soda in a cup holder, and kept the bag of pretzels in my hands, not quite ready to eat them yet, but having them ready for when I was.

"Thanks," I replied.

For at least several minutes, neither of us said anything. Jeff drove while I merely watched what was either a Milwaukee County sheriff's vehicle or City of Milwaukee police vehicle ahead of us, almost as though it were an official armed escort, out of the airport complex and onto the highway heading northwest. When our conversation started up, it took a different, though welcome turn, from what I would have expected it to start.

"So you're from the funeral home. How long have you worked there?" I asked.

"Long enough, a few years anyway."

"What made you want to get into this line of work?"

"Not quite sure how it started, but sometime in college I became interested in providing a service to the community, and this ended up being where my path led."

"Why Sparta?" I asked.

"I was born and raised there."

"Really," I replied, followed by, "What's your last name?"

"Schanhofer."

"Sounds familiar. What year did you graduate?"

"1995."

"Huh. Not sure why the name rings a bell then, as my family only moved to Sparta in '95."

"Might be because of my little brother. He used to play football for the schools there."

"Could be," I replied.

After a bit more conversation on this, we came to the conclusion that I probably did know his little brother, who graduated from high school somewhere between the three years that separated the years when Alex and I had graduated. After a while, our conversation diverged into other topics such as profootball, other sports, and the weather. At some point as we got farther northwest in the state, it started to snow, with some fairly big, heavy flakes falling down fast. This, I knew, was going to add to the already cold conditions I'd felt when I arrived in Milwaukee.

Around 11:30 p.m., we pulled off the exit on the highway that led to Sparta. The drive through the town, being dressed in a white, heavy snow, was a little over ten minutes long. After making a left into the parking lot, we drove around in a bit of a circle to bring the back of the hearse in line with the front door leading into the funeral home, underneath a bit of protection from an awning. As we did so, I could see the lights through the windows around the building, but particularly through the windows on the main doors into the building. I could see my family, all huddled together, apparently talking and awaiting our arrival. As we pulled up and parked, I prepared myself for what I knew was going to be a hard moment, among many others, in the coming days, but this evening was going to be particularly hard, as in less than half an hour, it would be Thanksgiving Day.

I took a breath as the hearse pulled to a stop, then, once I was sure it was parked, stepped out with my bags, and set them on the ground. I then went, along with Jeff, to the back of the hearse, where he opened the door and fiddled around with some of the security elements. The coffin came out about a foot or so from the back. A moment or so later, the honor guard was there, and with the warrant officer on one side, and me on the other, we both went to the position of attention. A minute or so later, the director of the funeral home itself came out with a mobile stand. The honor guard turned to face each other and very slowly and carefully, pulled the coffin the rest of the way out of the hearse, placing its center down on the mobile platform. Once they were sure that the coffin was balanced securely on the platform, the honor guard again took the handles along the sides of the coffin, and guided it inside. The chief and I held our salutes until the coffin had passed outside our respective lines of sight. I then picked up my bags, and went into the foyer of the funeral home. There were a few quick hugs from family as I placed my bags down out of the way of traffic, and then went into the room where the coffin had been taken. I approached the funeral home director.

"Excuse me, do you have a key?"

"Key?" he replied, somewhat confused.

"Yes, a key to open the coffin. Its official flag is inside, and I need to get to it."

"Oh, I see, yes, just give me a moment," he said, and then went off to get the key. The honor guard team was nearby when I had asked about the key, and when the staff sergeant acknowledged what we were talking about, he and another soldier went over to the coffin and very carefully, very deliberately, very slowly, lifted up the flag they had placed on it at the airport and then folded it up into the all too familiar shape of a triangle. The soldier then took the flag back to their vehicle.. A few minutes later, the funeral director was back. He found the right size key from a ring of similar keys, and then unlocked the coffin. The staff sergeant and I took out the flag, and carefully unfolded it from its secure triangular fold, carefully folded one time, and then placed it on the lower half of the casket, leaving Alex's upper body visible. I took a step back, and let Dad, my stepfather Brad, and my brothers, Dave (having made it home from his deployment to be here) and Bob, walk arm in arm to the casket to see what I'd already seen. Bob was crying, wailing quite hard. Dave had tears falling, but his cries were much more subdued. Dad looked crestfallen, but no tears fell from his face. Brad was similar in emotion to Dad. After a few minutes, both Dad and Brad looked back at Mom, and she took that as a sign to move forward. She went over to the casket, right in front of it, and Brad came over to put an arm around her to help support her if she needed it. Mom cried. All told, she probably took it better than the others had thought she would, whereas I had no idea what to expect of her reaction and just watched. It was now just after midnight.

Thanksgiving Day had come.

FOUR

Thanksgiving

Sparta, Wisconsin
24 November 2005

Mom was still looking at Alex, with my brothers, Dad, and stepfather close by. I took a step back to talk, once again, with the funeral home director. I told him that I needed him to review some forms, and add his part to the official record. This included things like whether or not more makeup was going to be needed. We stood there for a few minutes while he looked over the documents. Ultimately, his assistant, Jeff, the man who picked me up in the hearse in Milwaukee, was the one who filled the documentation out and signed his name to the forms. By the time this was done, everyone was moving back out into the hallway and the foyer. I got some more hugs, and one or two statements that still chill me to the bone. The basic sentiment of them was this: "Thank you for bringing him home." It gave and still gives me chills because, for a long time, I felt that I hadn't. Certainly I hadn't brought him home in the way everyone would have liked, hoped, and preferred. If I had, he wouldn't have been lying there, in a box, covered in an American flag. Despite the chill, I said nothing, merely nodded or redirected conversation elsewhere. The first question was where everyone was going to sleep. Bob would head back to La Crosse, and would meet us later in the day, at Mom's. Dave said that his (then) wife Dana was already waiting for him at Dad's house. For the time being, that was where I would head as well with Dave, but not quite right away. As we exited the building to get into cars and go where we needed to go, Dave stopped for a second. He turned to me, and then said, "You mind going for a bit of a drive?"

"Sure," I replied, as we took off. For a while, we just drove in the snow, commenting on how cold it was compared to where we had both just come from. After about a half hour or so, we ended up out by a field not too far from Dad's place. Dave parked with the engine idling, so that we could keep the heat going. Then he turned to me.

"So, I've got some questions to ask, if you don't mind and can answer them."

"Depends on what you ask," I said.

For about an hour, we discussed what the general situation was where I had just left, and what I knew, and could speak of, about what happened to Alex. According to my escort mission orders, I was not supposed to talk to the family members about what I knew of the injuries or the situation that had resulted in the death of their loved one. Because most escorts are just individuals selected for the task, and often have no connection to the families, this is a sensible rule easily followed. However, because I had seen what I had seen, and more importantly because I was family, I did what I could to bend, though not break, the rule in this one instance. Part of this was because Dave and I had things we knew about one another regarding our jobs that made it so that we were able to talk about these things without having to explain too much of the terminology or jargon that would have confused people. Moreover, I felt that in this one instance, he had as much right to know as anyone about what was going on and what had happened to Alex, given that both he and I were on our second deployments to the Middle East. The one question I remember for sure that he asked me, and that I answered within the bounds of regulation, was about improvised explosive devices, or IEDs, and I had explained to him the weird presentation of the military reporting of the incident since the event title had a question mark at the end, not knowing what kind of attack it had been. By 2 a.m., we both were ready for some much needed sleep, and drove the five minutes or so to Dad's place. Dave joined Dana on a fold-out couch while I settled down into either an inflatable mattress or a cot, I can't remember. We both dozed off as quickly as we could to get at least a few hours of rest before we had to tackle the rest of the day's activities.

Everyone started to stir after 5:30 a.m., with the last of us finally up around an hour or so later. The morning itself was slow.

People took turns using the bathroom, as there were so many of us. Dad had slept in his office, while one of his sisters, my aunt, as well as her husband, took his bedroom to sleep. Grandma had slept in her room. With Dave and Dana on the fold-out couch and me on an inflatable mattress or cot in the living room, there wasn't a whole lot of space for people to move as they awoke. After a couple of hours, the couch was folded back up and the cot/inflatable mattress was stowed away. Everyone had a quiet breakfast. There was little to no conversation, other than greetings from me to Dave's wife Dana, as well as to my grandmother, aunt, and uncle. Around mid-morning or so, Dave, Dana, and I loaded up his rented car and drove to where Mom and Brad lived, about forty-five minutes or so away, with traffic, stop lights, and snow, in La Crosse. When we arrived, we found a slightly more talkative atmosphere than the one we had left. Bob was there, as was my other grandmother, who came in by train not long after she got the news about Alex. Brad wasn't there that day; he was with his daughter, my stepsister, as she went through a surgery to correct an issue with her heart that had already been postponed twice. He would be back with us the next afternoon, after his daughter was out of surgery and safely in recovery.

Naturally, as we came in the door, there were hugs given all around. After which, Dave, Dana, and I set our coats down and out of the way. For a little while, the weather was discussed, as the snow from the night before had lessened but not yet completely stopped. During a pause, Mom left the room. When she came back, she had a package in her hand that had markings indicating something along the lines of overnight shipping.

"Here, Don, this came for you the other day."

I took the package from her hand, and noticed that while it had her address, it was addressed to me. I opened it up to find my unit patches and distinctive unit insignias. First Sergeant Collier's husband had indeed worked fast, as I now had what I needed to complete my dress uniform.

"Thanks, Mom," I replied, and then showed everyone what was in the package, quickly explaining why. At that point, with uniform instruments in my hands, I asked Mom where she had put Alex's dress uniform that he had left there before he had deployed. We went to one of the guest rooms, and found his full garment bag. I opened it up, and looked to make sure it had what I needed to make Alex's uniform complete. Sure enough, there were the necessary distinctive unit insignias, three of them, as well as what was referred to as a "flash" that went behind Alex's Air Assault wings. The flash colors vary, and identify the regiment a soldier is actively serving in. I knew back in Landstuhl there was no way Alex's uniform would be complete without that flash, letting everyone of us who would see it, which ultimately amounted to two people, know that he was a proud member of the Rakkasans, the 187th Infantry Regiment. I pulled all the necessary items carefully off the uniform and stuck them inside the package with the components for my own uniform, knowing that it was best to have them all in one place where I could find them. I then closed the garment bag, and went back into the living room to join everyone.

A little while later, there was a small discussion regarding the setup for the wake that coming Saturday. It was decided that an array of photos and photo collages would be set up for people to view on their way to see Alex's closed, flag-draped casket, and this would be followed by a receiving line, to meet the immediate family of the fallen. Us. This discussion didn't last long before we got into another one about music choices for the day of the funeral itself. With Dad not being there, I didn't know if this decision was going to be checked with him later, or if he merely deferred to Mom on this particular planning.

One song for the funeral had, ironically enough, already been decided upon. Mom told us this at the outset. One of us—either Dave, Bob, or myself—vocalized surprise at this.

"Really?"

"Yes," Mom started, followed by, "Alex actually picked it."

"He did?" one of us asked, sounding a little concerned on this point.

"Yep, on one of his last visits here."

"He did, huh? How so," I asked in reply, curious to hear the story.

"We were driving over to your Dad's to drop him off. As we listened to the radio, a song came on called "My Immortal" (by a band called Evanescence). It was a beautiful, but sad song, and at some point, I had to turn it off. I told Alex, 'That's a beautiful song, but it's a little bit too sad. It always makes me cry.' After telling him that was the reason I had to turn it off, Alex said, 'Yeah, I know. I can hear it being played at my funeral.'"

The room went silent for about a minute. No one said a word, but it felt as though everyone was in agreement on this. Alex, for whatever reason, felt as though he knew something. Therefore, we knew that the decision was made that this song would be played. No reason for argument was found by any of us, or if any had been, none was vocalized. One song down.

"Hey Mom, I've got a song I want you to hear, maybe we can use it as well," Bob chimed in, a bit of a sad, but hopeful look in his eyes.

He and Mom went over to her and Brad's computer, and Bob pulled it up. Mom put on some headphones, and for some minutes was just silently listening. The song Bob had picked was by artist Steven Curtis Chapman, though for the life of me, I can't to this day recall the title of it. After Mom was done listening to it, she turned to Bob and said, "It's nice." And that was it. No statement on whether or not we would use it or not. Just a simple note on it.

After a few quick moments of silence, Dave got involved in the discussion.

"Mom, I've got a song I want you to listen to. Maybe we could use it somewhere." Dave went over to where Mom was, and pulled up the song, and let her listen. The song was called "When I Get where I'm Going," a duet by Brad Paisley and Dolly Parton. Mom listened, and you could see there was a growing emotion in her. When it was over, she turned back to the group, and Dave began to tell the story of how this song came to him as one to possibly use.

"So, I was waiting in the airport for my flight to start boarding, and was listening to my MP3 player in order to keep my mind occupied. The player was on random. All of a sudden, this song comes on, and all the emotion I'd been holding in just let go. There's a line in there that makes me think of Alex being with Grampa, ya know. . . ." Dave grew silent, and Bob came up to give him either a hug or another consoling gesture. Conversation on song choices came to a halt at that point as we all just reminisced a bit about Alex. At some point later, it was

The four Gaunky brothers. Clockwise from top: Dave, Donleigh, Alex, and Bob. (*Author*)

determined that the song Dave had chosen would also be included in the funeral program.

Somewhere around 3 or 4 p.m., it was time for Dave, Dana, and me, as well as Bob, to get going. We all gave Mom and grandma, Mom's Mom who had come up, hugs, collected our jackets (as well as, in my case, the package of uniform materials) and left. Bob was coming with us to spend a little bit of time with Dad, our other grandmother, and some other relatives that night for a relatively small Thanksgiving Day meal. After about an hour or so of driving, Dave and Dana dropped us off, as they were going to visit a close family friend for the evening. Bob and I entered to see grandma, our aunt, Anne, and her husband Chuck sitting at the kitchen table. Dad was in his chair in the living room, which was separated from the kitchen by a couch.

We were told that the food had just recently been put into the fridge, and to go ahead and get something to eat. We both did so, and then ate in relative silence. There was no conversation during or after the meal that night. Not long after we arrived and started to eat, Dad went into his study where he ended up staying the rest of the evening. Around 8 p.m. or so, Bob and I set up our sleeping arrangements, one of us taking the inflatable mattress, the other taking the cot, and settled down to some reading. It was probably the first day I fell asleep during that period before 11 p.m.

The next morning was another early one, though without Dave and Dana, there were a couple less rotations to use the bathroom. Breakfast was a fairly quiet affair, though there was at least a bit more conversation than there had been the previous morning. I looked over my uniform pieces to ensure I had all the patches and parts I needed when I noticed something out of place. It turned out that while at the clothing and sales store in Germany, I had grabbed the wrong belt; I had picked up a woman's belt. There isn't too much different between the two, but those differences, mainly the length of the belt as well as its width, meant that when Dad and I went to the Post Exchange (PX) at nearby Fort McCoy somewhere between 9 and 10 a.m., I'd have to get the correct belt. I picked up everything else, placed it inside the garment bag, and waited to move.

Dad and I got into his old van and left the house somewhere around 8:30, and drove for about twenty minutes or so, and then after a quick check by the security guards, we were allowed entrance to Fort McCoy. Some minutes afterward, we made it to the PX and looked for the alterations shop inside it. The shop had been forewarned by one of the casualty affairs office representatives that we would be coming in for a rush uniform alteration. When I walked into the little shop, I mentioned who I was and briefly explained the situation to the individual working that day—"Black Friday" of all days—just to ensure they were aware of what was going on. Not long after that I was directed to a small dressing room where I put on the dress pants and jacket. After doing so, I stepped back out and was directed to stand wearing a pair of dress shoes on a box. I did so, and the lady marked the pants up for hemming, as well as where the patches were to go on my coat arms. I went back into the dressing room and carefully changed, came out, and handed off the items as well as the necessary patches to the alterations shop employee.

"How long do you think it'll take to make the alterations?" I asked as I was tying my shoes a bit tighter.

"About an hour or so. We'll put an announcement over the speaker system when we're done if that helps," she replied. I nodded and then stepped outside the shop into the main store area of the PX. I looked over to one side of the alterations shop to see a barbershop next door. Figuring that my hair was coming close to being out of regulation, and having time to kill, I went in and got a cleaned up high and tight. After paying, I went over to the portion of the store where they sold military uniforms, got the correct belt, paid for it, and then walked around the store while I waited to hear my name called. When it came, I was asked once again to put the dress pants and coat back on to see that everything came out alright. I did so, and after verifying that everything was good, I changed one more time and then paid the shop employee the cost of the alterations and patch work. Taking everything in hand, Dad and I went back to his van, and drove back to his house.

Shortly after we returned, Dad went into his office to check his phone for any messages while we were out. When he came back, he turned to me and said, "Hey Don, our congressman called for you while we were out."

"Called for me?" I replied. Dad nodded his head, and I let out a curious sigh, wondering what my congressman wanted to talk to me about. Surely, Mom and Dad were more important to talk to than me, as they were the ones making decisions related to funeral arrangements and the like. After a bit of questioning in my head, I let the concern of why he wanted to speak to me go to the back of the filing cabinet of my subconscious. I figured at that point, if it was really that important, he'd get a hold of me later.

Sometime around mid-afternoon, Dave and Dana came to pick Bob and me up to take us to the hotel where blocks of rooms had been reserved for family members to stay in during the wake and funeral period. Bob and I met Mom at the check-in desk, and filled out paperwork and had our information confirmed at the front desk computer. Not too long after, Bob and I were given our room keys—we would be sharing a room— and left to go put our respective luggage and clothes in it. For a little while, we just stayed in there and got our bearings, before deciding it was time to go to the hotel restaurant to meet and visit with family who were starting to come in, as well as with Mom, Dave, and Dana.

That night only a few of the aunts, uncles, cousins, and the like made it in. Conversation was light, over drinks of beer, wine, or preferred alcohol, for the adults anyway. The only real conversation of interest I found was the weather, as many of the relatives there that night weren't sure they'd make it in that evening because of the snowstorm they'd had or gone through on their travel up to Sparta from parts of northern Illinois. I ended up back in my hotel room sometime around 10 p.m., did some light reading, and then went to sleep, Bob coming in shortly after or possibly before that point. We both knew, along with most of the immediate family, that tomorrow was going to be a long day, and any sleep was going to benefit us. For in the morning, things were really going to get tough.

FIVE

Wake

Lanham-Miller Funeral Home
25 November 2005

Saturday morning went by a lot slower, and a lot later than the two mornings before. Instead of a 5 or 6 a.m. wake-up, it was closer to 7. I woke up before Bob did, and took care of necessary personal hygiene. As I walked out of the room to go to the restaurant and get some food, Bob finally started to stir. Breakfast that morning was a bowl of cereal, a glass of orange juice, and a couple cups of coffee. I sat and talked for a while with Mom and the one or two other relatives that passed through. At some point before 8:30, I saw Dave, and we talked about meeting up a bit later in the morning to get our respective uniforms, him his navy "crackerjack" uniform, and me the distinctive army greens, ready for the wake and subsequent funeral the next day. We set a time of around 10:30 or 11 to meet up in his hotel room. I finished up conversation and breakfast, and then went back to my room. I then turned on the TV, went over to my bag, and pulled out packs of ribbons and a ribbon rack, as well as all the other accouterments that go on any given army uniform. After setting most of these aside, I took the packages of ribbons and the ribbon rack, and carefully opened them up, trying to not damage the cloth of the ribbons as I did so. For the next half hour or so, I took my time putting the ribbons onto the ribbon rack in as correct an order as I could remember, in order of precedence from the upper left down to the lower right of the ribbon rack.

After making sure that this was done, and the ribbon cloth hadn't been torn by the metal backings or the ribbon rack itself, I set them aside with the other uniform attachments. I then pulled out a black wool beret from its plastic covering, and went over to the sink, where I proceeded to take a "fuzz" machine to it to make sure it was relatively smooth and free of pills. I then placed the beret under the faucet of the sink, doused it with water, turned the water off, and then placed the now wet beret on my head, shaping it to get it into its correct form. After letting it sit for a little while on my head, I then carefully took it off and let it hang from one of the door handles of the room to let it finish drying out. After that I would see if it needed any further adjustments. With a few minutes to relax, I changed the channel on the TV to something that would keep me entertained for a little bit while I waited for the right time to get ready for the wake, as well as to go to Dave's room to finish uniform preparations.

At 10 a.m., I changed into a white undershirt, placed my green dress pants, belt, black dress socks, and black plastic shiny shoes on. I then grabbed my dress shirt, carefully placed the shoulder boards onto their respective epaulets, went over to the mirror and carefully placed one of the two nameplates onto its correct pocket top. I collected the rest of my uniform pieces, and then went to Dave's room. I knocked a couple times before he opened it up. Dave was dressed in a white undershirt, his dark navy dress pants, and dress socks. He left his low quarters, the shiny shoes, off until he knew he'd have to put them on, as we'd likely be standing all day and those things don't take long to get uncomfortable. Over the next hour or so, we went back and forth on our respective uniforms, making sure awards and other things were aligned properly, while Dave's wife Dana sat in the background watching us pretend to be military efficient. Dave then put his crackerjack top on, and we got his neckerchief set up. I then put on my tie, placed my dress coat on, and we adjusted things as were necessary. When we were sure things were set correctly, I gave him thanks, as well as a hug, grabbed my beret and a few other things I'd brought with me, and walked out to the restaurant to grab something to eat before I got a ride, with whom I don't recall, to the funeral home.

The wake was supposed to start at 3 p.m., but the immediate family—Dave, Bob, Mom, Dad, as well as Brad, Dana, and others—and I wanted to get to the funeral home early in order to get a little bit of personal time before we had to be part of a

Alex in Kuwait before moving up to Iraq. He'd be dead within eight weeks of it being taken. This was the photo that accompanied the author's poem displayed at the wake. (*Author*)

receiving line for those paying their respects for our loss. When I got there, I met, for longer than a couple of minutes, the casualty affairs office representatives who had been assigned to Mom, Dad, and the family since the week prior, when Alex had succumbed to his wounds. Both were very good men, and, based on conversations I would have much later with Mom, Dad, and Brad, I was glad that they were the team there to support us. After visiting with them for a little while, I made my way over to the numerous photos and photo collages that had been strewn along the right side of the room in which the wake, and later funeral, were to take place. So many memories were accumulated in these images. One of the presentations meant more to me than I had time to speak of to family at the time.

The poem that I had sent back to family earlier in the week was on one side of a laminated print, with a picture of Alex in his military gear, in the desert at one of our camps in Kuwait that those of us who've passed through there know all too well. That particular image, and accompanying poem, encased in a frame, said a lot about who Alex was, or at least what I thought he was, around the time of his passing. I stood looking at it for a couple of minutes, somewhat transfixed by this reality before I eventually moved on to look at other photos, such as one of a young Alex standing triumphantly on his bike, hand on one of his hips, the other holding the handlebar of his bike, smiling the all too familiar smile that everyone knew him for. I couldn't help but smile a little bit. Dave and Bob and Mom and Dad also went around looking at the photos and photo collages, as we spent our time in relative silence, reminiscing in our own memories most likely. In a couple of chairs in the middle of the room, coming in probably forty or so minutes before the wake was supposed to begin, sat both grandmothers and Dad's sister Anne, watching us walk around the sides of the room.

At about twenty minutes out from the start of the wake, and our endless standing in line for a few hours, the casualty affairs representatives called us over to the left side of the room, not far from where we would be standing in our receiving line. Dad stood on the far right, followed by Mom and Brad (back in town after making sure his daughter's medical visit went well), Dave and Dana, Bob, and then myself on the far left. This order would be the same, but in the opposite direction, when the wake began. The two representatives told us that we were about to receive Gold Star lapel pins, items given to all next of kin—spouses, kids, parents, and siblings, along with stepparents, stepsiblings, legal guardians, or other such individuals who were integral parts of that individual's life. It was explained to us that this pin was to be worn on the lapel of any jacket or in a similar position on other clothing, in order to signify to others that we are relatives of a servicemember who died in war. Then one of the representatives called out loudly, "Attention to orders!" This is used at any presentation ceremony in the military to command servicemembers to stand in respect to those individuals receiving awards, promotions, or commendations. Dave and I, both of us being in uniform, went to the position of attention, and stayed that way, as the casualty affairs representatives went down the row and handed each of us a small box, within each was a Gold Star pin. Dave and I only relaxed a little when we had to put out our hands to receive our own boxes. After handing me mine, the representatives then came back in front of us, and released everyone who was at attention, which included the honor guard members as well as Dave and myself. They then returned to the background, and remained there in case we needed anything.

Mom, Dad, and Bob, as well as possibly the two grandmothers, who had been given lapel buttons from either Dad or Mom, pinned them to their left lapels. Dave and I could not do so, as we were in uniform, and the Gold Star pins were considered items of civilian wearing, and thus not part of either army or navy regulations. That said, Dave put his on anyway, nearby or on the tail of his neckerchief. I did what I could to put mine on as well, placing it on my tie below the line of vision, beneath my coat. It acted as a tie pin, even if it wasn't supposed to be or even technically count as one. At that particular point though, I didn't care. Neither did Dave. Both of us felt that neither of us were going to be the only ones unable to wear, and thus represent, ourselves as part of Alex's family. We were, to some degree, breaking regulations, but I'm pretty sure that neither of us in that moment particularly worried about that fact.

The wake started about five to ten minutes after 3 p.m. Part of the reason was the time it took to sign one of the books as you came into the funeral home. The other was the time it took people to walk around, looking at the photos and photo collages and then taking a few moments to themselves at Alex's casket.

Within the first group of twenty or so people that came to our receiving line was one of my cousins, and to my memory, one of Alex's favorite cousins, if not his most favorite, Brittany. Britt, as many of us tend to refer to her, was not quite nine months younger than Alex. As such, they were not only close in age, but, in all honesty, probably as close as extended family members could get. For a long time, when Alex was young, he had a huge crush on her, as cousins sometimes do. That crush evolved over time to a more sibling-like love. And it could be seen at this point while she was in line standing next to her mother, my Mom's sister, and my aunt. Both had tears in their eyes as they no doubt saw memories from not just Alex's past, but for their shared pasts. And while sad, it was good to know that they were here, as no doubt Alex would have been with them to comfort them if he could. Other family members were around them, and they too had signs of grief, or for some of the younger cousins, confusion. And this would present itself in the evening, as will be told later.

The line was fairly steady after our extended family members, with many of the people Alex had been close to during school not far behind. They, like our extended family, were feeling the loss significantly hard, and it was not difficult to understand why. These individuals, like Alex's friend Rachel, who many called by her nickname "Rae," had gotten to see Alex develop into the man he would become while his brothers, that is, Dave, Bob, and I, were away in the service, doing things that were difficult to conceive beyond what we told Alex in snippets when we had a chance to visit. Alex's friends got to help shape him in ways that we, being somewhat absent in his later teenage years, could not. Their grief was no less hard to watch as it was for family members, like Britt. When each of them got to us, it was, for me at least, bittersweet. Meeting—or in the case of many of the early visitors to the wake—reacquainting with people who were a part of Alex's life, was something very few of us would have fathomed happening. At least, not in this particular manner. Hugs and handshakes, and words of solace, or at least condolences were given for those who were not quite as well known to each of us.

After these first sets of groups, the line of people ebbed and flowed, and those who didn't leave after paying their respects, sat in chairs with either other family or friends who knew Alex and reminisced with old stories. As such, depending on the size and speed of the line, we—the immediate family members— would, as needed, take a break from standing in line. The only one of us who stood in the receiving line the whole time, whether there was a person coming on down the line or not, was Dad. Like a military officer or sergeant major holding down the fort, Dad was the constant in that line, even though I know that Dave, Mom, and I tried to do the same, but bathroom breaks or whatever other reasons didn't always make it possible.

Beyond the general ebb and flow of the line and the view of people sitting in chairs in the center of the room talking, three particular incidents stand firmly in my mind about the wake, and each of them surprised me and in some cases left me speechless. The first was somewhere in the middle of the wake, when an older gentleman who I didn't recognize came up to me after making his way past the pictures, the flag-covered casket, and other family members.

"And you are . . ." he started to ask, as though trying to remember himself who I was, as though we had met previously.

"I'm Don," I replied.

"That's right," he started, and after a pause said, "I'm Michael." He apparently saw a bit of confusion on my face, as though the phrase, "okay, and that matters why" were written in bold lettering. He responded to what I can only assume was a confused look with, "Grandpa Michael."

The moment between he giving me his name, and then adding the relationship aspect wasn't more than a second, but it was enough for me to take a step back internally, and probably revealed a shocked look on my face. Grandpa Michael was my Mom's father, and a man I hadn't seen at that point in time, in over ten years. It explained why I didn't recognize him. It would also explain the shocked look on my face, because I hadn't seen him for over a decade, and it was really, truly out of the blue that he would suddenly show at this point, after the death of his fourth grandchild, to become a part, once again, of his family members' lives. We talked a bit longer, and then he went on his way. While I never got much closer to him prior to his passing some years later, other family members did. This showed me that sometimes, in death, families who are somewhat strained or estranged can come back together.

The second incident that occurred was one that not only shocked me in its suddenness, but also in its innocence. After stepping out of the line at one point, Dana returned to where Dave and I were standing. At that point, the line had a significant break in it, and we were just waiting for it to come back around. Dana said to Dave, and to some extent me, something neither of us could probably have expected.

"Someone might need to talk to Wade," she started, followed by, "He just asked 'When's Alex coming out to play?'" The raw impact of that was pretty much immediate after she said it. Wade was, at that time, the youngest of our cousins on my Dad's side, the youngest child of his brother Scott. He was not much more than five years old. And in that sentiment relayed to us from Dana, it was obvious to me what it meant. No one had explained to Wade what had happened to Alex. My guess was that there were two reasons for not doing so. One, it would be hard for him to understand at so young an age. Two, if he did, it would be really hard for him to take. I don't recall ever telling Scott or Pam, Wade's parents, of this account. I've no idea if either Dave or Dana did either. All I know is that that expression of innocence was one which, for at least that moment, hit me hard and brought me out of the autopilot my mind had been on to get through this day.

The third and final incident is one that actually caused silence in the funeral home. It was fairly late in the wake, and the din of conversation by those who were still there was loud enough that it was sometimes hard to hear the person standing next to you. I don't even recall who I was talking to when all of a sudden, a voice carried out over the entire room, above all conversations and other background noise with a traditional command.

"Ten-Hut!" The silence after the command was given was immediate. Every single head in the room turned in the direction of the command, even with some of us going to attention ourselves, those of us in uniform anyway. At the front of the room, right in front of Alex's casket, was a group of what looked like bikers. And they were. They were members of the local American Legion Riders. Within seconds of the first command, and the following silence, came the next command.

"Present, Arms!" The entire group rendered slow, very pronounced, military salutes. Those of us in uniform followed suit. Everyone else merely watched in the silence. After about a minute or so of standing there, paying their respects, the commander of the element again gave out another set of orders.

"Order, Arms!" The group lowered in very slow, very coordinated movements, their arms from salute. Another minute or so of silence, and the group proceeded down to the receiving line, to us, the family of the fallen. It was only at this point that conversation picked back up to where it was before. It was there that people, who were happily reminiscing as though the one that was gone was still here with them, were brought back to reality. It was, in essence, a sobering moment. As the group passed, I made sure to shake hands and say thanks, and where possible give a supporting hug, to each member that came through the line. Having that kind of a response, and that element of respect, is hard to forget, and even more so one that will always remind me that servicemembers from the past will always take time to honor our own fallen. Always.

By the time the wake ended around 7 p.m., it had already been an emotionally exhausting day. It wasn't quite at the point where it would get any easier. As I walked out of the funeral home to get in the vehicle with family members to go back to the hotel, a car pulled up into the parking lot. Out of it stepped a man with older metal glasses frames and a carefully manicured beard. I knew the man, though we were not on close terms. He was the pastor of the local Methodist church, and had kids who we had gone to school with.

He started walking over to us asking, "Did I miss it?" He meant the wake. We told him that it had ended some minutes ago. He looked a little disappointed, but shook it off. We spoke for a few minutes, and then everyone proceeded to their respective vehicles to leave.

Immediately upon arrival back at the hotel, I went to my room and took my uniform off, carefully setting it aside for the next day, when I'd be wearing it once again. I changed into some PT pants, the green T-shirt I'd bought in Kuwait, comfy socks and tennis shoes, and, because it was still fairly cold out, my Army PT jacket. I then stepped out of the room and walked down the hallway toward the restaurant, both to get some food and, just as likely, to visit with extended family more than the few minutes we had to talk at the wake. When I got to the lobby, I noticed an individual looking as though he was trying to obtain information. The most distinctive feature he had was his high and tight haircut. That meant that he was either wondering where the local post was, not being from the area, or, just perhaps, he was looking for information about Alex.

"Hi," I said to him, before continuing, "You look like you're looking for something." I felt that I might as well state the obvious, as one can only go forward from there.

"Yeah, do you know where the visitation for Private Gaunky is, or if it has ended?"

Very few things surprised me by that point, but this was one of them. What were the odds of meeting someone looking for the wake of a recently deceased soldier?

"It ended a little while ago," I replied. I was going to ask who he was, but was cut off by a response from him.

"Damn. I was hoping I'd make it in time." After this, and a sigh, I got back on track to ask my follow-up question.

"Sorry, and you are?" I didn't mean to sound so direct or, perhaps, nasty with him, but given the long day, I wasn't quite in a place to be all together subtle.

"My name's Staff Sergeant Zuckerman. I was Private Gaunky's squad leader before the unit deployed." Very direct, no malice, no hint of frustration at being asked a somewhat stupid question. More importantly, this was one of the guys who knew Alex when he was at Fort Campbell.

"Oh, sorry if I was a bit rude there. My name is Don, I'm PFC Gaunky's brother." We shook hands. Over the next few minutes, we chatted away. I found out that he had been held back from the ongoing deployment because of medical issues, but prior to that, had been one of Alex's leaders. Moreover, just like the honor guard, he had driven all the way up from Fort Campbell to be at both the wake and funeral. Having missed the wake, I was sure there was no way he was going to miss the funeral. A few minutes later, we parted. Dad came down to the restaurant and ended up spending considerable more time in conversation with Staff Sergeant Zuckerman, and from conversations I've had with Dad since, I wish I had too.

Not long after leaving the restaurant, I saw my Dad's sister Lisa. We said hi, and as other family members such as Mom or Dave passed, Lisa mentioned having hard copies of the paper (the *New Sun* out of Waukegan, Illinois) that she and Dave had done an interview for earlier in the week. She mentioned that she'd have some to give to us later. There were appreciative responses, and slowly but surely, the families—both Mom's and Dad's—began to congregate in the restaurant area. Looking into the restaurant, I saw tables had been put together, and could see how the families, while in the same room, were separated. Mom's side of the family was off on the far right, while Dad's side was on the left side, at tables that ended about the middle of the room.

Over the course of a few hours, I bounced back and forth, trying to take in this visit while I had the time. I spent a while talking to Britt and her Mom, as well as the other cousins, aunts, and uncles on that side of the table. I then spent more time over by Dad's side of the family, sitting across from Lisa, who welcomed me with the customary nickname "Done-lee!" (as opposed to the normal pronunciation of my name, "Don-lee"), the same nickname my grandfather had. To my left was Dad's brother Mark. Between the two of us, we polished off three or four pitchers of beer that evening, with Mark, being unusually quiet for what I knew him to be, refilling each of our glasses if they ever looked on the verge of being empty. Conversation, for the most part that evening, was about the weather, and reminiscing about old times. The one topic that would come up from time to time over the course of the evening, though, was whether or not I'd have to go back to my deployment when this was over. It was usually only asked once per individual, but collectively got a little bit aggravating. I didn't explain to them that I had no choice in the matter, and that I wanted to go back to finish what I'd started this round. As such, much of my aggravation was due to my own lack of trying to get them to understand. Not that I ever said I was aggravated about the questioning to anyone. I put on, what I thought anyway, was the same old, straightforward, strong face for the evening.

Around 9 p.m., Grandma Kia, Mom's Mom, decided it was time to get some pictures of us. Mom, Dave, Bob, and I were prodded over to a corner so that we would all fit into the picture.

"Remember to smile," Grandma said, particularly to me, and then took a picture or two on her digital camera. After looking at what had been captured, she came back to me, and said, "Donleigh, smile—with teeth." I was not, and by and large am still not, an open mouth smiler. Most of the pictures, for all of Grandma Kia's prodding, would demonstrate this. In a couple of the photos, we would see that our cousin Jordan, from Mom's sister Peggy, had gotten in the glass behind us in the corner and ended up photobombing the pictures. They made the pictures amusing. Grandma got into a couple of them as well. After everyone was content that sufficient pictures had been taken, some family members went back to talking, others to their rooms to get some sleep.

Somewhere around 11 p.m., I had a quick discussion with Dave about getting to the funeral home a bit early the next morning, as I wanted to put the last minute touches to Alex's uniform, the distinctive unit insignias and flash, before the ceremony. Getting there before others would make it easier, and also make it so that nobody else had to see the extent of his injuries. After agreeing on a meet-up time in the lobby, I wished him a good sleep, said goodnight to the family members still in the restaurant, the majority already having left for the evening, and then went to my own room to get some desperately needed sleep for what I knew was going to be a long, hard day, and the last day of this mission.

SIX

Funeral

Lanham-Miller Funeral Home and Leon Cemetery
26 November 2005

My alarm clock buzzed around 5:30 a.m. After turning it off, I spent a couple of minutes with my eyes open, staring at the ceiling, then out the window. Finally, I got up. I showered, shaved, and took my time putting my uniform back on, as I knew, as with yesterday, today was going to be a long day. I did my best not to disturb Bob during this time. On walking out of the room, beret as well as black leather dress gloves in hand and Alex's uniform parts in my coat pocket, Bob finally started to wake. I walked to the restaurant, found an open table and chair, took my jacket off, and carefully placed it on the seat back next to me, and set my gloves and beret onto the seat itself. I went and got a cup of coffee, as well as a bit of food from the complimentary breakfast line. Very few people were up and stirring at this point. My guess is that, like me, they knew what was coming, and were trying to hold off having to manage their emotions. I went back to the table and drank my coffee and ate what I could. The whole time, I was watching the TV, which this early, had the local news on. The story playing when I sat down was the return of a Wisconsin unit from deployment. Local politicians were being interviewed, including the congressman who had tried to get a hold of me the Friday before. I knew, or had a least heard, that Mom didn't want him involved in the wake or funeral. She didn't want him to use it as some kind of photo op. Nevertheless, when he got done talking about the return of the unit, he mentioned Alex's funeral, and said something about the cost of war. Even without being allowed to attend, he had still gotten his photo op. I let it pass, as I was not in the mood for being angry at that point.

I finished my breakfast fairly quickly. After throwing my plate away, and pouring another cup of coffee, I went back and sat down to watch some more news. At some point, I saw Mom come in to get breakfast. I let her know about the report I'd watched. She told me someone had told her about a similar broadcast the previous night, which she had missed, and that she'd try to find it when the news repeated itself a little later in the morning. She continued to get her breakfast, and I continued to sip my coffee. I sat there and drank my coffee waiting for Dave to come down. We had discussed the night before about going over to the funeral home early and finish making sure Alex's uniform was complete. While waiting, Staff

Sergeant Zuckerman came out to the main lobby and restaurant entrance. Like me, he was dressed up in his Class As, the only difference between us was that he had shined airborne boots on instead of the glossy low quarters. As a member of the 101st Airborne, he was authorized to wear them in dress uniform. We greeted one another, and he went quickly to get some coffee. Upon his return, I told him about going to the funeral home early to make sure Alex's uniform was complete, and he asked if he could come with, as he needed to know how to get to the funeral home anyway. I said I had no problem with it, and that we'd just need to talk to Dave when he came down.

Time passed, and as it got closer to the time when Dave and I had agreed we would depart for the funeral home, there was still no sign of him. I got anxious. I went to his room, and knocked on the door.

"Just a minute," he said, and then opened it. He saw me in uniform, and then must have realized what time it was, as the words that came out were, "Ah, shit. I forgot." He was dressed in a white undershirt and pair of shorts, but no uniform yet. We talked briefly, and I let him know about Staff Sergeant Zuckerman's wanting to come with us. I let Dave know that I would just catch a ride with Zuckerman to the funeral home, and get the task done. I would then meet up with him when he got there. Somewhat somberly, he agreed. I could tell he wasn't at all happy that he'd forgotten what we had talked about, but I wasn't going to sweat it much. I walked back to the lobby, talked with Staff Sergeant Zuckerman about the plan, and we took off from the hotel to the funeral home.

It was a cold morning. Very few people were out and about. There was a mist-like fog in the air. We took all of maybe fifteen minutes to get from the hotel to the funeral home. We parked his rental vehicle in a corner of the parking lot, and walked into the funeral home. I talked with either Jeff or Mr. Miller about opening the casket so that we could make final corrections to Alex's uniform. After about a minute or so, one of them came back, and unlocked the casket. Staff Sergeant Zuckerman and I carefully folded the flag back, and then opened the lid that covered the upper half of the remains, the part we would need to work on. Zuckerman took a distinctive unit insignia from me and put it on one of Alex's epaulets while I put one on the other. I then gave him the flash to put behind Alex's air assault wings while I took the last unit insignia and tried to fasten it to his beret.

It should be noted that most soldiers are not dressed with berets on in their caskets, but because most of the injuries were to Alex's head, they made the exception in this instance. I carefully tried to move the beret up just enough so that I could feel the cardboard backing on the opposite side of the beret's flash where I would be able to push the insignia's pins through. The beret, however, was difficult to move sufficiently to do this, so I had to lift it, as carefully as I could, higher to get it a little more off his head. As I did so, I got a better view of his injuries. I tried to act as fast as I could so that I could put the beret back down, but every time I tried, the beret was still not high enough to put the insignia in properly, and I'd have to pull a bit rougher to get it to come up higher. Every time I did, more and more of his injuries became visible. I finally got it high enough to start putting the pins in, but as I was doing so, my eyes became partially fixated on the injuries I saw. I finally had to turn away, because the sight affected me greatly. The only way I can describe what I saw is to use a movie reference, that being the top and back of Darth Vader's head after it had been burned. That is about as close as I can get to describing it, and it was enough to actually affect me emotionally, more so than at any other time in the last nine or ten days. My only solace was that Staff Sergeant Zuckerman had completed putting the flash underneath the air assault wings, and was in a position to temporarily take over. I came back to help him complete the task after turning away for about ten seconds. Once we were sure the pins were secure and not going to cause any further damage to Alex, we set the beret back in its original position. We closed the lid, and carefully drew the flag back over the casket. Either Jeff or Mr. Miller returned, and locked the casket. The final touches were now complete.

At this point, Staff Sergeant Zuckerman wandered over to look at what was left of the photos and pictorial collages on the right side of the room. I looked around to get my bearings and tried to get a sense of how the funeral would play out. In the room, the chairs from the previous evening remained set up into three sections, left, middle, right. Across the front rows of the right and middle sections were tape and papers designating them as reserved seating. One would think that the middle section of reserved seating would be for the immediate family of the fallen, but in this particular instance, our seating was the reserved section of the right wing of chairs. Odd, I thought. Who else could possibly be seated in the middle section up front and center, closest to the coffin? Not knowing who it could possibly be, I let that thought, for the time being, slip to the back of my mind. Looking over to the left wall, I saw a piano or keyboard, as well as a microphone stand. Must be for live singing, I thought, though I couldn't think of when that decision had been made. Probably before I got back, I said to myself. Having gotten a reasonable understanding of the layout, I decided to walk around as well.

As time passed, people started to arrive at the funeral home. The casualty assistance officers got there, as did other members of the military services, mostly from the army as that was Alex's branch. Family members also started to arrive, Dave finally in a place where he was okay, and in his full crackerjack navy dress. The official party, that is a general officer from the branch of service of the fallen servicemember, arrived. In our case, it was a major general, or two star in military parlance. Generally speaking, the official party is a high-ranking individual, usually a general or an admiral, there to represent that service in paying respects to the family of that individual. Accompanying him were several colonels, at least one major, a captain, a sergeant major, which is one of the higher senior enlisted individuals in an army unit, and other servicemembers scattered about. There was also the honor guard from Fort Campbell, which to my mind, was really the only other military people around besides the casualty assistance officers that I had any interest in seeing or talking to at that point. Too much brass, or officers, as it were. Being a junior non-commissioned officer, I, as well as others I have known, tended to follow a general rule of avoiding such rank unless officially required to.

At some point before the room really started to fill with people, I was informed, along with other immediate family members, that we would be receiving official copies of the executive order issued by the governor of Wisconsin that directed flags to be flown at half mast today. The governor would not be there himself to give the copies to us, so we would receive them from the lieutenant governor in his place. At that time, we were told that she had not yet arrived, and that we would hold the presentation of the executive order as soon as she did. There was some concern, though not quite vocalized strongly, that she might end up being late and arrive after the funeral service had begun. We would, at that point, only know for sure when she got there.

Time continued to plug away, and the funeral home room was finally starting to look as though it would be completely full by the time the service started. When it was just a little under an hour left before the service, Dad, Mom, Brad, Dave, Dana, Bob, and I were brought to a little room in the back, where the casualty assistance and other officers were settled. We were still waiting on the lieutenant governor to arrive, when the major general decided there was other business that could be handled. As the rest of us watched, Mom and Dad were brought forward, and turned to face the rest of the people in the room.

"Attention to Orders!" an aide carefully bellowed out. Anyone and everyone in the room that was in a military uniform snapped to the position of attention. One by one, both Mom and Dad were presented with Alex's earned honors, as well as orders and certificates to go with them. Purple Heart. Check. Bronze Star. Check. Iraq Campaign Medal. Check. Good Conduct Medal. Check. These were presented in order, and great care was given to ensure they were delivered with respect. By the end of the awards ceremony, which is what this little event amounted to, Mom and Dad each had several boxes that contained a medal, ribbon, and lapel pin as well as several presentation holders for the certificates that came with them. Their hands were essentially full.

"At Ease!" We relaxed. At this point, we were presented with another item for the family. The football team for the local high school every year at their awards banquet presents what they referred to as the P.R.I.D.E. Award, given out for special recognition to an individual who contributed significantly to the team in that particular season. Somehow, it was determined that Alex, even though he had graduated over a year prior, would be the recipient of the award that year. After these presentations, we remained in the room, waiting for the lieutenant governor to arrive, or for the funeral service to start, whichever came first.

Time ticked away, and as it came to a point where the brass were simply going to let us go out and start the funeral on time, the lieutenant governor finally arrived. After a quick shake of hands, Dad, Mom, Dave, Bob, and I were each presented with a paper copy of the declaration signed by the governor ordering flags to be brought down to half staff in recognition and remembrance of Alex. The little ceremony lasted about five minutes or so. After which, we set the documents and awards aside, and stepped back into the main room where the funeral was to be held.

Where it had been partly full when we had left to go into the small back room, the hall was now not only filled to capacity, but dozens of people were standing along the back wall and entrance to the room. The family went to the reserved area designated for us on the right side of the room. Dad was on the far right side, followed by Mom and Brad, Dave and Dana, Bob, and then finally me at the left end of the row, right next to one of the aisles separating the right and center sections, and for me, sitting across the aisle from the lieutenant governor. To her left were all of the other brass, settled in, somewhat uncomfortably from the looks of many of them, right in front of the coffin. At that point, it hit me that that was who the other reserved section had been held for, though I was still not entirely sure why, nor why they were closer to Alex than we were, but with music coming in and a notice that the ceremony would be starting shortly, I put it out of my mind and turned my face to the podium off to our left, near Alex.

As with most ceremonies that have any kind of religious context, particularly funerals, this one started out with a prayer, followed by words from the presiding military chaplain, a colonel from the local military post, Fort McCoy, where Dad and I had been two days ago to have my uniform altered. After a few more words, intended to comfort, we came to a musical interlude, with, I believe, "When I Get where I'm Going," playing first. While listening to the song play, I could also hear the very noticeable sound of tears and crying occurring throughout the room. It was noticeable, it was palpable. And yet, ironically, I gave away no sentiment of sadness, certainly not outwardly. Off to my right, Bob was very open about his grief. He seemed to be very much affected by the music. When the song was completed, more words were again spoken, and touched upon the fact that Alex was no longer suffering here on earth, or something to that effect. And then once again, there was a musical interlude, "My Immortal" played over the sound system of the funeral home. This time, emotions were very high for people. Bob in particular seemed to take it very hard. He bent down in his chair, and his cries were very loud. Mom, even though she was saddled with her own grief, quietly got out of her chair and crouched in front of Bob, holding onto his hands and head while he let loose the torrent of emotions he was feeling. At the same time, and slightly before Mom got up from her chair, I was taking my right hand and trying to pat his back in an attempt to console him. It took to the end of the song for both Mom and me to get Bob to calm down enough for things to move forward.

More ceremonial rights were given, and then we got into what I consider the last, pertinent, musical interlude. My cousin Brendhan was over at the microphone on the left side of the room I'd seen earlier, and a middle-aged woman sat at the piano. Somewhere in the planning, likely while I'd been in Germany, he had been asked to sing for the funeral. The song choice was "The Lord's Prayer." When he started out, there was a slight crack in his voice, most likely hit with the emotion of what was going on around him. It didn't take him long to move past it, and by the time of the third word in the song, he was hitting it out of the park. The accompanist, not so much. I'm not sure if she was playing in the wrong key, or if the piano was out of tune, but at some point, she simply stopped playing, letting Brendhan sing most of the song a capella. Perhaps, in my view, that's how it should have been anyway. Just a family member, singing out in a way I've never heard equaled, either in terms of sound or the emotion it carried. When he finished, while still a somber and quiet type of event, if one discounts the tears and cries, it was probably one of the better moments of the day.

Following Brendhan's tribute, the eulogy was presented. Selected for this task was one of Alex's favorite teachers, Cale Jackson. Mr. Jackson taught math at the high school we went to, though he arrived after Dave, Bob, and I had left school. Only Alex was taught by him. I had met him twice, both times when I was on leave and Alex had invited me to come with him to his chess club meeting, which Mr. Jackson was the adviser. Mr. Jackson wasn't a particularly large, physical individual, but there was no doubt that he was a man of intellect. He was also a man of heart. His eulogy, which talked about Alex being part of a team, and how that was what he wanted to be, not a star, just a member, described Alex to a T. He talked about the different things that made Alex who he was and why being part of the team was enough for him. He also mentioned Alex's smile, and his way of trying to get people inspired or involved, from dancing break dance moves at school dances to making sure the football players had their water when they came off the field after a down was completed. The line that got people to laugh was when Mr. Jackson said Alex wouldn't want us to be down and have somber, sad music playing, but rather he'd want us to stand up and dance. And it was true, he would have wanted that. The eulogy went on for about twenty minutes or so, but it was by far, apart from Brendhan's singing, the most appreciated and most needed by all those in the room, including family, to pay our respects.

The eulogy over, our time for the memorial at the funeral home was essentially complete. All that was left was for us to go to the cemetery to perform military honors and rights. That would require us to get out of the building first, which apparently was the plan from those in charge. Almost.

"Ladies and Gentlemen," announced the director of the funeral, "this concludes this portion of the funeral ceremony, the rest being at the cemetery where military honors will be rendered. You are invited to attend there as well. We just ask that you allow the family members and VIPs to exit the building first before everyone else so that we can begin the funeral procession to the cemetery. Thank you."

VIPs? The word rattled around in my head. What VIPs? The only VIP for this thing is, and should only be, Alex, encased within his coffin. I knew I wasn't the only one puzzled by this sentiment. There was a murmur going around the room as my parents, brothers, and I got up and turned to head out to the main foyer, and the vehicles waiting outside. I got one look back over to the other reserved section, and could see signs of frustration in the eyes and faces of most of the military brass. Clearly, they weren't happy with the phrase and sentiment of being "very important persons" either. If I had to guess, the sentiment was dropped in to allow the lieutenant governor the chance to vacate and leave without being pestered by those attending. That's just my guess though, but would be partly supported in the fact that she was not at the cemetery when the military honors were rendered about a half hour later.

Dave and I were among the first people outside. He traversed over to my left side, and we ended up being back probably about a dozen feet or so from the rear door of the hearse, which was only a few feet away from the building's entrance. We waited. As we did, many of the people from inside the funeral home either came around behind us, or stayed where they could see on either side of the back of the hearse. The last group to come out was the honor guard, guiding the coffin out of the building almost exactly the same way they had brought it into the building four days earlier. When there was a clear enough view that they were actually exiting the building, Dave and I, without saying a word to each other, went to the position of attention. From somewhere behind us, we heard someone sound off with, "Ten-Hut!" Then someone called out, "Present, Arms!" Dave and I raised our right hands carefully into very stiff, very straight salutes. Neither of us had said anything about doing this when they were going to bring Alex out to the hearse, we just did it. Almost directly behind us, Aunt Lisa captured on her camera, or possibly camera phone, an image that she would share with everyone later. It was a picture of Dave and me, our backs to the camera, arms up in salute. Between us in the background can be seen the honor guard, carefully placing Alex's flag-draped coffin into the hearse. It is a powerful photo, and to this day I'm not entirely sure how she was able to capture, without first being overcome with emotion, something that is so indelibly imprinted on my mind from another perspective.

The honor guard moved the casket slowly into the hearse, as they were taking such care with it. At the same time, the funeral home driver ensured that it was securely fastened with each step the honor guard took placing it in the hearse. As the casket was moved out of each pair of soldiers' hands, from back to front, they went to the position of attention, and when the last set of hands let go of the coffin as it finally sat on the back floor of the hearse, all of the honor guards saluted. They then took a step or two backwards, and the hearse door was closed. Everyone who was saluting carefully and respectfully started to lower their arms, the command of "Order, Arms!" coming from behind us again.

The crowd started to disperse, more than a few to get into their cars to be part of the funeral procession over to the cemetery. I walked over to Dad's van, which was the first vehicle

The author, right, and his brother Dave saluting Alex's flag-draped casket. (*Lisa Sears*)

behind the hearse. After a few minutes, with people getting settled into their vehicles and getting them started, we began to drive out of the lot. We made a right turn out of the parking lot following the hearse and the local police at the front of the procession providing escort. What I saw, and everyone behind us saw, was something unexpected. On turning that corner, we found that all along both sides of the road were people holding up American flags. Parents. Kids. Veterans who broke out their uniforms and put them on in order to pay their respects. It was completely different from what happened when I rode with Staff Sergeant Zuckerman to the funeral home that morning. The streets had been empty. Now they were packed with people. As we drove through the downtown area on our way to the cemetery, I remember seeing a couple of old navy petty officers wearing their uniforms, clearly veterans as they had mustaches that were way outside of regulation. It didn't matter, the fact that they decided to do like so many others, and put on their uniforms as a sign of respect, was enough. About halfway out of town, we came across a small group of individuals watching us going by, one of them, elderly with a wheelchair, was standing up and saluting, regardless of whether doing so was inadvisable. The man, probably a vet, still decided to stand, and salute. I couldn't help but feel a kick to the chest, my stomach knotted from these displays, overwhelmed.

About twenty minutes or so later we arrived just outside the cemetery. We made a left turn and crossed over the street onto the main dirt road that ran through it. We circled around until we were on the north side of the cemetery, the vehicles facing in a northwest direction. Dad stopped the vehicle some feet back in order to give the honor guard room to carefully bring the coffin out of the hearse and carry it over to a little tent-like cover with a green material covering the ground around the grave hole and the chairs which fell under the cover. Dad went over to the structure, while I walked over to where the major general, chaplain (a colonel), and honor guard officer in charge were standing just a few feet back from the vehicle on its right side. We stayed there for a while as the honor guard marched over to the back of the hearse. The back door was opened. Slowly, steadily, carefully, the honor guard lifted and removed the flag-draped coffin from the hearse, walking in lock step, left, right, left, right, to bring the coffin out. Once it was secure in their hands, they turned, with the chaplain walking in front of them, guiding them over to the spot where the final rights and military honors were to be presented. I walked behind for a while, and then drifted off to be by my family, just making it in time before the honor guard brought the coffin before us. Extended family members pointed me to the one unoccupied seat in the front, where the rest of my immediate family, Dad, Mom, and Brad, Dave and Dana, and Bob were still standing. Once again, as the coffin came in front of us, Dave and I saluted. We stayed that way until the coffin was placed upon the stand provided for it. The honor guard, once sure the coffin was secure, took a step back, and saluted as well. Then, all but two left our line of sight.

We sat for a little while, as the chaplain said some more words and a prayer. After several minutes, two members of the honor guard still in our immediate vicinity went over to each end of the coffin, and carefully lifted the flag off of it. Over a period of several minutes, they folded it, first in half, then in half again, both times leaving long but thinner lengths of the flag held parallel to the ground. They then folded it numerous times until it came to the all too familiar folded triangle. After ensuring that it was secured properly in its shape, the flag was placed inside of a triangular box, with Alex's name, rank, and birth and death dates etched into a metal square on top. The box was then closed, and another member of the honor guard received it from the two folding it. The soldier then turned and handed the tri-folded flag to the general, who then walked over to Mom, bent down on a knee, and said, "On behalf of a grateful nation . . . ." Mom took the box into her arms and held it for a little while, and then set it in her lap. An identical box was then presented, and the general who had bent down before Mom, did so now before Dad. "On behalf of a grateful nation . . . ." Dad took the box, and carefully placed it in his lap. The general then stood up, and carefully walked off to the side.

In the background, the sound of Taps could be heard. Usually, Taps is performed in an enclosed space where the sound bounces off the walls and therefore sounds as though it is repeating. Either that, or two buglers play it in staggered pattern. Here, in the cemetery, there was no enclosed space, no walls to bounce off of and echo in a repetitious pattern. Moreover, there were no multiple buglers to play the song. Just my cousin, Brendhan, essentially doing double duty in rendering his honors in music, and military honors in Taps, to a beloved cousin. When the first note of the bugle hit, everyone not already standing did so. Dave and I, and everyone in uniform within the sound of the song, went to attention and then immediately went into a salute. And we held it there. Just as Taps was winding to a close, the sound of rifles going off could be heard. I twitched and reacted to every one of the three volleys of seven shots fired. My mind was still in hyper-vigilance mode, only having left a war zone where such sounds were all too familiar a little over a week ago. I twitched and shivered, but I never dropped my salute, not until both Taps and the twenty-one-gun salute was over.

After several moments of silence, I brought my arm down. A quick word was said about how this was the end of the military honors portion of the funeral, and where the post-funeral luncheon would take place. I stepped over to the side for a minute, and then was handed a rose from my Dad's brother Scott. I knew what it was for. I joined in the queue of immediate family members as they stepped forward to place their rose on top of the coffin, their last words, prayers, and memories to be given in respect. When my turn came, I carefully leaned over the coffin and placed my rose on top of the other roses that were on a relatively flat part of the coffin at its center. I then placed my hand on it, said a little prayer, took a step back, and then rendered a solitary salute. After about twenty seconds, I dropped my salute, touched the coffin one more time, and then stepped aside. My mission to bring my brother home, to be both a brother and a soldier, a military representative to the family of the fallen, was now over.

Epilogue

It's been over ten years since I went through this almost surreal, seemingly impossible experience. And since that day, numerous things have changed, in me, and in life. Moreover, there are several things that have had an impact on my life, both in the almost immediate and short term events that followed my escorting Alex home, along with several issues I had to see and resolve in myself in those years. Some realities of this event, and a few other ones in its aftermath that I will shortly tell you, have opened my eyes. Others merely reinforced understandings that I'm loathe to encounter again. Yet all of them have played their part in affecting me in the aftermath of my mission, and my loss. And I will start by discussing three events that happened shortly after my mission to bring Alex home.

The one that was of greatest significance to me was a wake I went to a little over two weeks after we placed Alex on those support beams which would inevitably lower him into his final resting place. The wake was for a marine, killed by an IED four days after we buried Alex. He had significantly more time in the military than either Alex or myself, and yet there he was, killed by an IED in Anbar Province, Iraq, trying to add to the mission we had all been trying to accomplish. His wake was on December 14, two days before I would fly out to resume my deployment. For the third time in almost a month, I donned my army dress uniform, to pay respects to a man I'd never met, and to a family now similar to our own. When we (Mom, Brad, and I) arrived, there were cars parked all over the place, requiring us to park away from the church. The inside of the church was packed. We were in line for quite some time before we came in front of the marine's family. Mom had her Gold Star pin dutifully on her lapel, visible to anyone who would look. The fallen marine's family had been putting on strong faces with those that came before us in line. Those strong faces broke when we came before them. For they then knew that they were not alone in their grief, that there were others like them who understood. Mom and their family members cried together. I, for whatever reason, remained relatively stoic, or more likely dispassionate, in my disposition. After a small commiseration, I walked over to where the coffin lay, flanked by two Marines providing guard and honor for one of their own. Being there reinforced my need and desire to return to my deployment. To be able to do my job and ensure as many of my brothers and sisters in arms would return home upright. So that there were fewer families who would have to endure what we and the marine's family were having to go through at that moment. That notion of honor to my siblings in arms, whether fallen, wounded, or relatively unscathed has remained to this day, even though I no longer wear the uniform of a soldier.

The second event, which actually happened before the marine's wake, was a call I got the day after we placed Alex in the cemetery ground. That phone call came from my congressman, who had been unsuccessful in reaching me before the funeral. On checking out of the hotel on the Monday after the funeral, I went to Dad's house to spend some time with him, which I would split with Mom, before returning to Iraq. Not long after we got there, Dad's phone went off, and he went into his office to retrieve and answer it. When he came out, he turned to me.

"Don, it's the congressman. He'd like to speak with you."

I was as perplexed as I had been a few days earlier when Dad had told me about the call I'd missed. However, I figured there must be a reason for him to want to talk to me, and took the call to find out why. "I'm going to go take this in your office," I told Dad right after he handed me the phone, him nodding to me after I gave my reply.

"Sergeant Gaunky?" he asked.

"Yes?" I replied, and he identified himself as a congressman.

"I wanted to talk to you about some things, but before I do, let me offer you my condolences for your loss."

"Thank you," I replied, not sure where this was going.

"Did your travel back home go okay?" Odd question, but perhaps he'd just been concerned I wouldn't make it home for the funeral, I thought.

"Yeah, it was okay, a little long though."

"I can believe that." This statement was followed by a long pause, as though he were formulating what it was he was going to ask me, or attempting to figure out the best way to ask it.

"So, do you still work in intelligence?" Again, an odd question. I'd met the congressman several times in the past, though only once since I joined the service, and that had been when he visited Mosul in 2003 while I was on my first deployment. I don't recall ever telling him what I did for my military vocation, so it is entirely possible he read about it in all the local media that surrounded Alex's passing. Still, for whatever reason, I answered him.

"Yes," I said, somewhat hesitantly, again not entirely sure where this was going.

It was then that he started asking me what I can only describe as "policy" questions, such as: "How do you think the (parliamentary) elections (in December) will go?" "Do you think the local security forces will be able to handle things during the vote?" These and similarly focused questions are what he asked me for probably about ten to fifteen minutes, while listening to my responses to them. Somehow, despite the grief that I was dealing with, I was able to coherently answer his questions to the best of my ability. Even more surprising, looking back on it, was my capacity to not delve into or provide classified information to him in providing such answers. How I was able to do that in the state I was in, I'll never know. After finishing up his questions, we said our goodbyes.

It was not until over a year later that I realized what had happened, and the seeming callousness and coldness of the situation. I emailed the congressman a few times over the years since then to find out how he felt asking such questions at an inappropriate time. I never got an answer, just a form letter that gave a generic apology for anything he may have said that had offended me, not realizing it was the timing of his call and not necessarily its topic that was offensive. The incident left a bad taste in my mouth. I got the feeling from him, both from his call and later when seeking an explanation for it, that he either never really cared, nor understood, what his responsibilities were regarding foreign policy or their impact on people here at home. Since then, I have always wondered how many other politicians have done that, or something similar to it. That interaction left me with a disdain for politicians of all stripes.

The last event in the days following the funeral that had a long-lasting impact on me was my return to Iraq. I returned to, and finished, my deployment as was my duty. My second one no less. I have to admit that I did not do so in the best of states though. Not long after my return, I had a conversation with Captain Bryant, asking to see if it was possible for me to go "outside the wire," meaning out of the base where the war was actually taking place. I asked to be able to do it just once during this deployment. Not on a helicopter flying over the city. I wanted to be in a vehicle on the ground. I wanted this for two reasons. The first was to truly understand how things were going beyond the reports I'd been reading day in and day out. It's one thing to read reports and try to understand. It's another to actually be on the ground and get a true understanding of what the lay of the land is. Moreover, I wanted to see if things were improving, not just for servicemembers working in theater, but for the people we were there to help. The average, everyday Iraqi who couldn't leave after being there for twelve months. The ones for whom the land was their home. The second reason was to see if all the sacrifices made, from those in my unit during my first deployment, to those going on when I returned for a second time, and in particular because of Alex, had been worth it. I knew I wasn't going to see that through reports, but had to be on the ground, outside the wire, like I'd been dozens of times during my first tour to Iraq.

The response I got from Captain Bryant was not the most conciliatory of answers. "We'll see." Basically, it was about as close to a "no" as I was going to get. Whether or not she pursued the question, she was not the final say in the matter anyway. Had my unit not done what it would do during the remaining ten months, I probably would have been okay with that response. Not happy, to be sure, but content. Over the rest of the deployment though, my unit, when not on our shift hours, would conduct combat training on the sentiment that, paraphrasing here, "We could be called out for a mission at any moment, so we have to be ready." That training was busy work. And it made me angry, to the point where, for a long time, I was somewhat resentful towards my higher command for "jerking my chain." I knew we weren't ever going to go outside the wire, and they probably knew it too. I can understand Captain Bryant's likely reasons for giving me a noncommittal answer, being that I might either fly off the handle and hurt one of the locals or that I myself would become a casualty, another flag to give to parents and family members already in mourning. That said, I was not a fan of the unit pretending we were preparing for combat. I basically stewed, for the most part, during the rest of that deployment. I was also not in a healthy position. My sleep cycle went off kilter. My work performance, as a consequence, was also faltering, to the point where I was no longer a supervisor of soldiers, and my task was shifted.

The only bright spot during that deployment, besides having support from Captain Bryant and Staff Sergeant Thai, even when they probably shouldn't have been giving it to me, was numerous pep talks from an older, salty marine major that started occurring about two or three months after my return, when the major replaced another marine we had been working with earlier in that deployment. The man, Major Rayfield, would give me periodic motivational talks about things such as me carrying on the guidon, or flag, for my family and my family's service. The major helped me to keep working, and do what I'd set myself out to do following my recent experience in the States. The major's talks, and the aforementioned support from my two immediate supervisors, sustained me enough to make it through to the end of my deployment. Not in good shape, mind you, but certainly better than I would have been without them.

I returned from that deployment, by and large, otherwise unscathed, certainly at least physically. Over the next two years, I was on edge as talk would come and go about whether or not our unit would deploy again. My reason for this was twofold. First, it would determine the time frame in which I would begin to start the process of exiting the army. Normally, provided you aren't retiring, that process is supposed to begin a year out from your last contractually required date. That would have put me at about early summer of 2007 to begin that process. If we were deploying, I wanted to know, so that I didn't start something I would have to stop, and then start over later. The second reason, and in some respects, the more important one, was if we were going to deploy, I was going to need the time to prepare my family for that reality. It would, had it occurred, have been my third deployment, and the seventh or eighth one my parents and family would have had to endure since my oldest brother Dave had joined the military in 1999. The reason I say seventh or eighth is that Dave, too, was in the same boat, as the navy might have scheduled him for another tour to the Middle East during most of that same time period. Neither of us knew for sure. Nor was I sure how it would impact Mom, Dad, and the rest of the family, to once again roll the dice, and thus potentially have another family member come home in a flag-covered box. Ultimately, we would not deploy for a third time.

The biggest positive during those years came toward the end of them, when a regulation was changed for the better. In February 2008, the army decided to allow individuals who had received the Gold Star pin as a result of a family member lost during service to wear it on their uniform. Officially. Or rather, almost everyone. When my first sergeant at that time, First Sergeant Chandler, brought me down to hand me the notification of the change, I was happy, particularly now that I could be somewhat whole, and represent Alex with me when I wore our dress uniform. Then I read the change, and found a huge hole.

"I still can't wear it," I told Chandler. He looked at me a little flabbergasted.

"What do you mean you can't wear it?"

"Siblings are not included on the list—see," I said, as I pointed it out to him. If I was depressed about this fact, Chandler was angry. After confirming the rules as written were in fact not allowing me to wear the lapel pin, Chandler and I talked a few minutes more, and then he left.

Not long after, he pointed this out to Command Sergeant Major Scalf, our unit's senior enlisted soldier. He would then use this fact, and his understanding of my reality, to get the regulation changed so that all those eligible to wear this emblem, which signified such great loss, would be able to do so. Not long after, during a dress uniform inspection, in which Scalf reviewed us, he informed me that my uniform was not up to par. He then handed me the updated regulation message. It stated that siblings, including step- and half-siblings, now were able to wear the lapel pin on their uniform as prescribed. At my last uniform inspection and formal military event, I wore my lapel pin without trying to find ways to bend the rules, as I had since I had gotten it the day of the wake. Command Sergeant Major Scalf's actions, and my story, had helped to right a wrong.

I would return to visit Alex three times after that deployment when I escorted him home. The first was on my leave post deployment. It was my first time there with the headstone now in place. Dave was there with me. It was a quick visit. The second time was in June 2008, right as I was transitioning out of the military. Dad was with me on that venture, and it too was a short visit. The third time was during Memorial Day weekend in 2015. It was my first visit in seven years. Before that, I had little to no desire to go. I didn't want to because it was a reminder of the broken promise I'd made Mom before Alex and I had left for our respective deployments in the late summer/fall of 2005. That I wasn't able to bring him home alive. For so long, I had significant survivor guilt, even though I'd internally and intellectually processed the fact that there wasn't anything I

The author visiting Alex's grave. (*Author*)

could have done. There was always the lingering "what if?" in its numerous variations flying around in my head. Up until that 2015 visit, those what ifs were hard to get past. They have since become manageable, and the guilt not as hard to endure.

That guilt, besides the difficulties of trying to transition back into civilian life, and the suicidal episodes that came with attempting to do so, have been the most difficult things for me to deal with and address over the past decade. They still are at times, but they've been tempered enough to be able to deal with when they flare up. Those, the distaste for politicians, and the somewhat incomplete closure from the deployment because I could not go outside the wire one more time are the things I've carried with me since that mission. Since that loss. As such, they have made both the military and veteran side of my life and the Gold Star and survivor side of my life inextricable. I cannot separate those aspects, and thus am never completely comfortable with either sitting exclusively on its own. In past conflicts, the Civil War, World War II, Korea, such a reality or occurrence—a brother bringing home a brother killed in war— was much more common. Today, it is a rarity. It is such because public opinion and the laws created in response have made it so. And though rare, my situation, and the mission that ensued, does happen from time to time in the current state of modern warfare, where siblings must bring home their own. This story, and my reality, are proof of that. As are the consequences I explained above that come with it.

Acknowledgments

No book is ever completed by an author themself. While an author may be the one who initiates and writes the manuscript, there are so many other people who help guide the project to its final state. This book is no exception. Thanking everyone surrounding the writing and completion of this project would easily be a book in itself. As such, I find that I have to keep the thank yous down to those who were essential, in more than a few ways, to making this possible.

First, I'd like to thank Bruce H. Franklin and his crew from Westholme Publishing for taking this on and helping me to bring this story to life. The support, suggestions, and guidance given to me from you and your team have not only been invaluable, they have been nothing short of life giving during this process. For that, I cannot begin to thank you enough, but I hope that this is at least a start.

To my friend David R., for reading through part of the early draft manuscript and giving me MANY constructive criticisms and suggestions. This book would not be what it is today without them. To John F., for the most complete reading of the draft manuscript, and for your friendship and support. You're probably the closest person I know to have dealt with what I have laid out in this book, and for that we will forever remain brothers.

To the several Gold Star Siblings, mostly sisters, who were there when I first came out of the shock and were there to support me in the early days. Casey, Ami, Andi, Amanda, Katy, and brother Chad, you are all always in my thoughts and heart. To the other Gold Star Sibling, much more recently, for whom mutual support has been received and given; Patty, you are one of the bright lights in the day.

To Jen C. and Dani K., two friends, brought together by different losses, who were there when I needed help while in the darkness; you're both always in my heart. To my day-job co-workers Sue M. and Mark W. Thanks for the encouragement and support, and for occasionally listening to me ramble on about this project. To Sandy, Ike, Caleb, Allan, Jon K., HM Gautsch, and Beth aka "The Diva" for always being there. To Sheila, for keeping me on the right path and focused. To Dana T., you may no longer officially be family, but you will always be considered family to me.

Finally to my family. To Dad and Lisa (stepmother), thanks always for the encouragement and support. To Mom and Brad, thanks for the open ears and wide range of talks. To Bob, just because. To Dave and Alicia (sister-in-law), for all the support and love given over the years. To my niece Alexia and nephew Sammy, for the smiles and unconditional love; I hope you can one day understand your weird uncle when you read this. Lastly and most importantly, to Alex. Even though you're not physically here anymore, you are always in my heart and in my mind, and I hope I was able to be as good a brother to you as you were to me.